BTEC Level 3 National Study Skills Guide in Applied Science

Welcome to your Study Skills Guide! You can make it your own – start by adding your personal and course details below...

Learner's name: _____

BTEC course title: _____

Date started: _____

Mandatory units:

_____

_____

_____

Optional units:

_____

_____

_____

_____

Centre name: _____

Centre address:

_____

_____

_____

Tutor's name: _____

Published by Pearson Education Limited, a company incorporated in England and Wales, having its registered office at Edinburgh Gate, Harlow, Essex, CM20 2JE. Registered company number: 872828

Edexcel is a registered trademark of Edexcel Limited

Text © Pearson Education Limited 2010

First published 2010

19   18

18   17

British Library Cataloguing in Publication Data

A catalogue record for this book is available from the British Library

ISBN 978 1 84690 563 6

Typeset and edited by Ken Vail Graphic Design, Cambridge
Cover design by Visual Philosophy, created by eMC Design
Cover photo/illustration © Corbis: Gabe Palmer
Printed and bound by L.E.G.O. S.p.A. Lavis (TN) - Italy

Acknowledgements

The author and publisher would like to thank the following individuals and organisations for permission to reproduce photographs:

Alamy Images: Angela Hampton Picture Library 19, OJO Images Ltd 92, Stuart Walker 12, Claudia Wiens 74; **Corbis:** 84; **Getty Images:** Science & Society Picture Library 58; **iStockphoto:** 57, Chris Schmidt 33; **Pearson Education Ltd:** Steve Shott 28, Ian Wedgewood 67; **Science Photo Library Ltd:** Geoff Tompkinson 59

All other images © Pearson Education

Every effort has been made to contact copyright holders of material reproduced in this book. Any omissions will be rectified in subsequent printings if notice is given to the publishers.

Websites

Go to www.pearsonhotlinks.co.uk to gain access to the relevant website links and information on how they can aid your studies. When you access the site, search for either the title BTEC Level 3 National Study Skills Guide in Applied Science or ISBN 9781846905636.

Disclaimer

This material has been published on behalf of Edexcel and offers high-quality support for the delivery of Edexcel qualifications.

This does not mean that the material is essential to achieve any Edexcel qualification, nor does it mean that it is the only suitable material available to support any Edexcel qualification. Edexcel material will not be used verbatim in setting any Edexcel examination or assessment. Any resource lists produced by Edexcel shall include this and other appropriate resources.

Copies of official specifications for all Edexcel qualifications may be found on the Edexcel website: www.edexcel.com

Contents

Popular progression pathways

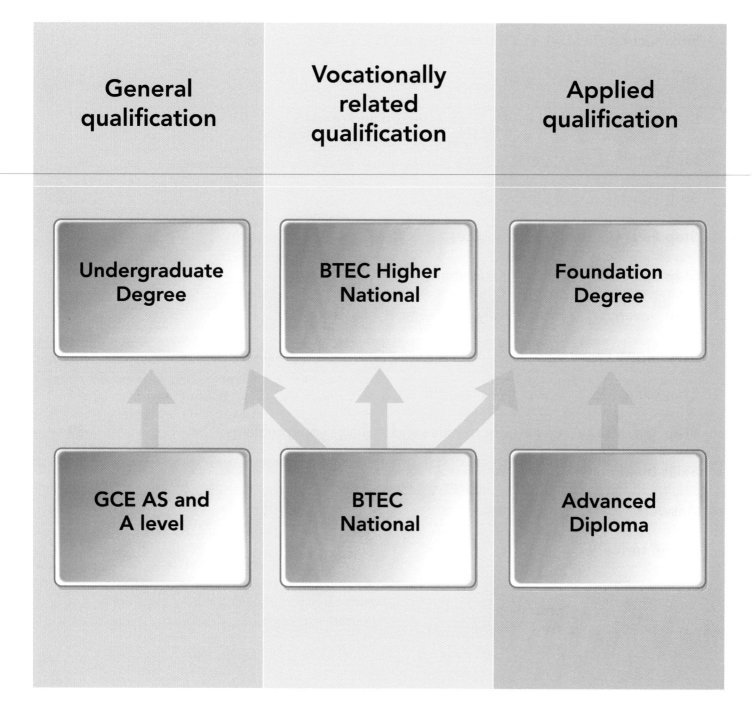

Ten steps to success in your BTEC Level 3 National

This Study Skills Guide has been written to help you achieve the best result possible on your BTEC Level 3 National course. At the start of a new course you may feel both quite excited but also a little apprehensive. Taking a BTEC Level 3 National qualification has many benefits and is a major stepping stone towards your future career. Using this Study Skills Guide will help you get the most out of your course from the start.

TOP TIP

Use this Study Skills Guide at your own pace. Dip in to find what you need. Look at it when you have a problem or query.

During **induction** sessions at the start of your course, your tutor will explain important information, but it can be difficult to remember everything and that's when you'll find this Study Skills Guide invaluable. Look at it whenever you want to check anything related to your course. It provides all the essential facts you need and has a Useful terms section to explain specialist terms, words and phrases, including some that you will see highlighted in this book in bold type.

This Study Skills Guide covers the skills you'll need to do well in your course – such as managing your time, researching and analysing information and preparing a presentation.

- Use the **Top tips** to make your life easier.
- Use the **Key points** to help you to stay focused on the essentials.
- Use the **Action points** to check what you need to know or do next.
- Use the **Case studies** to relate information to your chosen sector and vocational area.
- Use the **Activities** to test your knowledge and skills.
- Use the **Useful terms** section to check the meaning of specialist terms.

This Study Skills Guide has been designed to work alongside the Edexcel Student Book for BTEC Level 3 National Applied Science (Edexcel, 2010). This Student Book includes the main knowledge you'll need, with tips from BTEC experts, Edexcel assignment tips, assessment activities and up-to-date case studies from industry experts, plus handy references to your Study Skills Guide.

This Study Skills Guide is divided into ten steps, each relating to a key aspect of your studies, from understanding assessment to time management to maximising opportunities. Concentrate on getting things right one step at a time. Thousands of learners have achieved BTEC Level 3 National qualifications and are now studying for a degree, or building a successful career at work. Using this Study Skills Guide, and believing in your own abilities, will help you achieve your future goals, too.

Introduction to the applied science sector

The BTEC Level 3 National in Applied Science course provides you with the skills and knowledge underpinning all aspects of science. It does this in a work-related context in order to help you progress in your chosen career or onto higher education. It can help you obtain the grades to go on to study at university in a wide range of science-related subjects. These may include:

- forensic science
- chemical engineering
- biomedical science
- human physiology
- other biology, chemistry, physics or environmental-related degrees.

The choice of degree depends on the BTEC National course you have chosen to complete. Many universities state an overall merit grade as a minimum entrance requirement for science-related degree courses.

This course also provides you with valuable work-related experience and opportunities to practise the skills that are essential for any science-related job.

Depending on which course you take, you will specialise in certain areas of science. In all BTEC Level 3 National in Applied Science courses you will become confident in planning and performing a range of scientific practical investigations and evaluating your findings. You will also gain valuable knowledge of health and safety issues, maths, English, IT, and personal, thinking and learning skills.

You will complete assignments based on scientific job-related scenarios, for example working as a scientific researcher or producing material for public information in the science industry or NHS. Other skills you will gain include researching, preparing and giving presentations, and producing scientific reports following practical investigations.

A qualification in the BTEC Level 3 National in Applied Science can lead to a variety of jobs including work in:

- the pharmaceutical industry
- the health professions
- scientific research
- the National Health Service
- the environmental agencies
- the science industry.

You may also be qualified to work in research and educational institutions or for the government doing research and development, or scientific analysis.

The pharmaceutical, and food and drink industries, as well as many other sectors, have job opportunities for which you will be qualified.

You can even specialise in areas such as forensics or medicine, allowing you to progress onto a university degree in your chosen science-related field of study.

The qualification titles covered in the BTEC National in Applied Science are:

- BTEC Level 3 Certificate in Applied Science
- BTEC Level 3 Subsidiary Diploma in Applied Science
- BTEC Level 3 Subsidiary Diploma in Applied Science (Medical Science)
- BTEC Level 3 Subsidiary Diploma in Applied Science (Forensic Science)
- BTEC Level 3 Diploma in Applied Science
- BTEC Level 3 Diploma in Applied Science (Medical Science)
- BTEC Level 3 Diploma in Applied Science (Forensic Science)
- BTEC Level 3 Extended Diploma in Applied Science
- BTEC Level 3 Extended Diploma in Applied Science (Medical Science)
- BTEC Level 3 Extended Diploma in Applied Science (Forensic Science).

Activity: Your course

Now look at the specification for your particular BTEC Level 3 National in Applied Science course using the Edxecel website. Go to www.edexcel.com.

Make a list of the units you will be studying.

Skills for your sector

You will be expected to use some or all of the following skills when completing assignments for your BTEC National in Applied Science.

Health and safety, and housekeeping

These skill areas involve making sure the workplace is kept clean, tidy and free from any hazards caused by machinery, electrical equipment or chemicals; essential good practice in all science-related jobs. For example, microbiologists must work safely, keeping their working environment clean. They must carry out procedures correctly in order to prevent the escape of dangerous microorganisms that could cause health problems to themselves, other work colleagues and the public.

Activity: IT skills

Complete the following table to say how these IT skills could be useful in a science-related job.

IT skill	Science-related job	Why is this an essential skill for the job?
internet-researching skills	forensic scientist looking for secondary data on a forensic science technique	
saving files	biomedical scientist working with patients	
retrieving files	cancer research scientist working on a cure for brain cancer	
security	working for the NHS inputting patient data following treatment for HIV	
emailing	promotion officer working for the environmental agency	
producing PowerPoint presentations	public liaison officer working for the NHS in the immunology department	
using Publisher, Excel and Word packages effectively	clinical research scientist in a pharmaceutical company looking at a new drug to treat Parkinson's Disease	

Activity: Filing your work

Good filing means keeping all your work in one place so that you are organised. Create a menu page based on the template below for the particular BTEC National course you are doing.

Colour code each unit title and use matching colour-coded file dividers for each unit in your folder. Place the menu page in the front of your folder to create a working file where you can keep your Applied Science work safe and in order.

BTEC Level 3 National Applied Science file menu		
Introduction		
Safety info		
Unit number	Title	Tutor(s)
Unit 4	Scientific Practical Techniques	Miss Arthur
Other work		

Presenting your work

Depending on the requirements of different assignments, your BTEC National Applied Science course work will have to be presented in many different ways, just like the work of scientists in the real world. You may be asked to explore different presentation styles in some science-related scenarios like these:

- Acting as a public liaison officer working for the NHS, produce a presentation for the public on the spread of an infectious disease.
- Acting as a research physiologist, write a scientific report on an investigation into the effects of exercise on heart rate and breathing.
- Acting as a scientific writer, produce an article for a scientific magazine on the use of stem cells.
- Acting as a technical artist, draw and label cells you have identified under a microscope.
- Acting as a microbiologist experimenting to identify a cure for certain diseases caused by bacteria, produce the data for evidence.

English language

It is important that you have good English language skills.

- You need to be able to understand what you are reading, select appropriate information and then express it correctly. This process will help you to understand the science you are reading and to pass the grading criteria successfully.
- You need to be able to write good English in order to complete explanations, essays, reports and presentations, for example in a scientific context.
- Copying others' work directly is dishonest, so you need to learn to select appropriate scientific information and then put it into your own words.

Referencing your work and creating a bibliography

Referencing is a very important part of this course. You need to make sure that you state the sources of information that you have included in your work; copying others' work is plagiarism for which most centres have severe penalties. There are different ways to reference your work and your centre will tell you what system you are expected to use.

Find out which referencing system you will be using on this course by asking your tutor and make notes on how to do this for different sources of information, eg books, websites, newspaper articles, journals and information from television programmes or DVDs.

When you get your first assignment brief from your tutor, go to the library and/or use the internet. You will need to find some sources of information like the ones listed below. To be truly useful, these must be related to the assignment that you have been given.

Some examples of information you might need to reference could include:

- a website you have used to research a diagram on the structure of the nervous system
- a book you have read about how to do an investigation into enzyme activity
- a newspaper article that you have used as a source of information about current issues surrounding the spread of MRSA in hospital wards
- a journal containing secondary data on the effectiveness of gene therapy to treat cystic fibrosis sufferers.

Maths skills

On the BTEC Level 3 National in Applied Science course you will probably perform some quite advanced mathematical calculations. These will vary according to the particular course you have chosen. You could be required to:

- use a scientific calculator
- collect and analyse both primary and secondary data
- use the correct SI units when handling data
- present data in the appropriate graphical form
- for some course units, calculate chemical equations or perform physics calculations
- interpret both your own data and graphical evidence, and that of others.

Have you learnt any of these skills before and, if so, how confident are you?

Tick the ones that you are good at and put a cross against those which require further knowledge or practice.

TOP TIP

You can ask your tutor for help with any mathematical calculations that you have not done before, or find difficult.

Step One: Understand your course and how it works

Case study: Choosing your Applied Science course

Mohamed loves watching 'Crime Scene Investigation' on television and is really interested in becoming a forensic scientist. For this reason, he has decided to study on the BTEC Level 3 National Diploma in Applied Science (Forensic Science).

Before enrolling, Mohamed researched the BTEC National and local centres that offer it. He checked that it would give him the necessary UCAS points to get into university. He also made sure that he would find the course content interesting, and that it would be useful to him in the future. He discovered that he would have the opportunity to take part in a work placement; work experience will be very helpful to him when he starts looking for a job.

Mohamed is very happy with his choice of course and college. He is looking forward to the course work, including some work-related practical experiments and written assessments from which he can learn valuable skills.

He has made a note of the units he will be studying on his two-year course. This enables him to prepare by reading about some of the content he will be expected to cover for his assignments. His list of mandatory units is:

Unit 1 – Fundamentals of Science

Unit 2 – Working in the Science Industry

Unit 3 – Scientific Investigations

Unit 4 – Scientific Practical Techniques

Unit 5 – Perceptions of Science

Unit 6 – Using Mathematical Tools in Science

Reflection points

What do you think is the difference between studying for the BTEC Level 3 National Diploma in Forensic Science and studying exam-based qualifications?

How do you think work experience and doing work-related assignments might help you?

Activity: Your future options

At the beginning of a new course it is helpful to think about what career pathway options may be available to you in the Applied Science workforce. All assignments and work experience on the programme contribute to your final grade and knowing what you are aiming for will help keep you motivated.

Using a mind map to explore different ideas is a good way to consider the range of options available to you. You will also be able to find out the requirements for each career pathway.

For example, if you wish to work in forensics, you could explore the different routes to becoming a forensic scientist.

You will find the internet a useful source of information. A good starting point is the *New Scientist* website. Go to page 104 to see how to access a useful website for this activity. Use a mind map to record your ideas.

All BTEC Level 3 National qualifications are **vocational** or **work-related**. This means that you gain specific knowledge and understanding relevant to your chosen area. It gives you several advantages when you start work.

For example, you will already know quite a lot about your chosen area, which will help you settle down more quickly. If you are already employed, you become more valuable to your employer.

Your BTEC course will prepare you for the work you want to do.

There are four types of BTEC Level 3 National qualification: Certificates, Subsidiary Diplomas, Diplomas and Extended Diplomas

	Certificate	Subsidiary Diploma	Diploma	Extended Diploma
Credit	30	60	120	180
Equivalence	1 AS-level	1 A-level	2 A-levels	3 A-levels

These qualifications are often described as **nested**. This means that they fit inside each other (rather like Russian dolls) because the same units are common to each qualification – so you can progress from one to another easily by completing more units.

TOP TIP

The structure of BTEC Level 3 National qualifications means it's easy to progress from one type to another and gain more credits, as well as specialise in particular areas that interest you.

- Every BTEC Level 3 National qualification has a set number of **mandatory units** that all learners must complete.
- All BTEC Level 3 National qualifications include **optional units** that enable you to study particular areas in more depth.

- Some BTEC Level 3 National qualifications have **specialist pathways**, which may have additional mandatory units. These specialist pathways allow you to follow your career aims more precisely. For example, if you are studying to become an IT practitioner, you can choose pathways in Software Development, Networking, Systems Support or IT and Business.

- On all BTEC courses you are expected to be responsible for your own learning. Obviously, your tutor will give you help and guidance when necessary but you also need to be 'self-starting' and able to use your own initiative. Ideally, you can also assess how well you are doing and make improvements when necessary.

- BTEC Level 3 National grades convert to UCAS points, just like A-levels, but the way you are assessed and graded on a BTEC course is different, as you will see in the next section.

Key points

- You can study part time or full time for your BTEC Level 3 National.

- You can do a Certificate, Subsidiary Diploma, Diploma, or Extended Diploma, and progress easily from one to the other.

- You will study both mandatory units and optional units on your course.

- When you have completed your BTEC course you can get a job (or **apprenticeship**), use your qualification to develop your career and/or continue studying to degree level.

- On all BTEC Level 3 National courses, the majority of your learning is practical and vocationally focused to develop the skills you need for your chosen career.

Using the Edexcel website to find out about your course

- You can check all the details about your BTEC Level 3 National course on the Edexcel website – go to www.edexcel.com.

- Enter the title of your BTEC Level 3 National qualification in the qualifications finder.

- Now find the specification in the list of documents. This is a long document so don't try to print it. Instead, look at the information on the units you will be studying to see the main topics you will cover.

- Then save the document or bookmark the page so that you can easily refer to it again if you need to.

Action points

1 By discussing with your tutor and by exploring the Edexcel website, find out the key information about your course and use it to complete the 'Important Information' form on the next page. You can refer to this form at any time to refresh your memory about any part of your studies.

   a) Check whether you are studying for a BTEC Level 3 Certificate, Subsidiary Diploma, Diploma, or Extended Diploma and the number of units you will be studying.

   b) Find out the titles of the mandatory units you will be studying.

   c) Find out the titles of the optional units and identify the ones offered at your centre.

   d) Check the length of your course, and when you will be studying each unit.

   e) Identify the optional units you will be taking. On some National courses you will do this at the start, while on others you may make your final decision later.

   f) Find out other relevant information about your BTEC Level 3 National qualification. Your centre may have already given you details about the structure.

   g) Ask your tutor to help you to complete point 10 on the form. Depending on your course, you may be developing specific additional or personal skills – such as personal, learning and thinking skills (PLTS) and functional skills – or spending time on work experience, going on visits or doing other activities linked to your subject area.

   h) Talk to your tutor about point 12 on the form as your sources of information will depend on the careers guidance and information at your centre. You may find it useful to exchange ideas with other members of your class.

	Important information on my BTEC Level 3 National Course
1	The title of the BTEC Level 3 National qualification I am studying is:
2	The length of my course is:
3	The total number of units I will study is:
4	The number of mandatory units I have to study is:
5	The titles of these mandatory units and the dates (or terms) when I will study them are:
6	The main topics I will learn in each mandatory unit include:

	Important information on my BTEC Level 3 National Course
7	The number of optional units I have to study is:
8	The titles of the optional units I will study are:
9	The main topics I will learn in each optional unit include:
10	Other important aspects of my course are:
11	After I have achieved my BTEC Level 3 National my options include:
12	Useful sources of information I can use to find out more about these options include:

2 Many learners already have information, contacts or direct experiences that relate to their course. For example, you may have a specific interest or hobby that links to a unit, such as being a St John Ambulance cadet if you are studying Public Services. Think about the relevant sources of information you already have access to and complete the table below.

My information sources	
Experts I know	(Who they are, what they know)
My hobbies and interests	(What they are, what they involve)
My job(s)	(Past and present work and work experience, and what I did)
Programmes I like to watch	(What these are, how they relate to my course)
Magazines and/or books I read	(What these are, examples of relevant articles)
ICT sources	(My centre's intranet as well as useful websites)
Other	(Other sources relevant for my particular course and the topics I will be studying)

Step Two: Understand how you are assessed and graded

Case study: Thinking about grading and assessment

Jake and Sameer are both studying on the BTEC National Diploma in Applied Science (Medical Science). They were asked what they understood about how they would be assessed and graded during the course. Their responses are set out below.

Jake: 'I have carried out a lot of research using the Edexcel website into how we are assessed. I was a bit confused so I contacted my tutor, who explained it fully to me.

My understanding is that I have to show specific knowledge when completing my assignments, which can be practical investigations, case studies or presentations, for example. I have to make sure that I complete the learning outcomes for pass, merit and distinction for each assignment. I need to be independent in my approach, completing my work and handing it in to set deadlines.

I want to go on to university to study pharmaceutical science after this course, so I need to make sure that I get at least a distinction grade overall. This converts into the 360 UCAS points I need for the university course that interests me. I am going to design a form to record my grades as I go along. Then I'm going to convert the unit points I get into UCAS points, so that I make sure I get the grades I need.'

Sameer: 'I'm a bit confused about exactly how I will be assessed and graded during the course but I know it is all based on course work. I suppose the tutor will let me know what I have to do. I haven't looked at any university courses yet but I think I want to do something to do with scientific research.'

Reflection point

Have you thought about how you will be assessed and graded?

Your assessment

This section looks at the importance of your assignments, how they are graded and how this converts into unit points and UCAS points. Unlike A-levels, there are no externally-set final exams on a BTEC course. Even if you know this because you already have a BTEC First qualification, you should still read this section as now you will be working at a different level.

Your learning is assessed by **assignments**, set by your tutors. You will complete these throughout your course, using many different **assessment methods**, such as real-life case studies, **projects** and presentations. Some assignments may be work-based or **time-constrained** – it depends very much on the vocational area you are studying.

Your assignments are based on **learning outcomes** set by Edexcel. These are listed for each unit in your course specification. You must achieve **all** the learning outcomes to pass each unit.

TOP TIP

Check the learning outcomes for each unit by referring to the course specification – go to www.edexcel.com.

Important skills to help you achieve your grades include:

- researching and analysing information (see page 71)
- using your time effectively (see page 25)
- working cooperatively as a member of a team (see page 65).

Your grades, unit points and UCAS points

On a BTEC Level 3 National course, assessments that meet the learning outcomes are graded as pass, merit or distinction. The different grades within each unit are set out by Edexcel as **grading criteria** in a **grading grid**. These criteria identify the **higher-level skills** you must demonstrate

to achieve a higher grade (see also Step Six: Understand your assessment, on page 35).

All your assessment grades earn **unit points**. The total points you get for all your units determines your final qualification grade(s) – pass, merit or distinction. You get:

- one final grade if you are taking a Certificate or Subsidiary Diploma
- two final grades if you are taking a Diploma
- three final grades if you are taking an Extended Diploma.

Your points and overall grade(s) convert to **UCAS points**, which you need to be accepted onto a degree course. For example, if you achieve three final pass grades for your BTEC Level 3 Extended Diploma, you get 120 UCAS Tariff points. If you achieve three final distinction grades, this increases to 360 – equivalent to three GCE A-levels.

Please note that all UCAS information was correct at the time of going to print. However, we would advise that you check their website for the most up to date information. See page 104 for how to access their website.

Case study: Securing a university place

Chris and Shaheeda both want a university place and have worked hard on their BTEC Level 3 Extended Diploma course.

Chris's final score is 226 unit points, which converts to 280 UCAS Tariff points. Shaheeda has a total score of 228 unit points – just two points more – which converts to 320 UCAS points! This is because a score of between 204

and 227 unit points gives 280 UCAS points, whereas a score of 228 to 251 points gives 320 UCAS points.

Shaheeda is delighted because this increases her chances of getting a place on the degree course she wants. Chris is annoyed. He says, if he had realised, he would have worked harder on his last assignment to get two points more.

You start to earn points from your first assessment, so you get many benefits from settling in quickly and doing good work from the start. Understanding how **grade boundaries** work also helps you to focus your efforts to get the best possible final grade.

You will be able to discuss your learning experiences, your personal progress and the

achievement of your learning objectives in **individual tutorials** with your tutor. These enable you to monitor your progress and overcome temporary difficulties. You can also talk about any worries you have. Your tutor is one of your most important resources and a tutorial gives you their undivided attention.

You can talk through any questions or problems in your tutorials.

Key points

- Your learning is assessed in a variety of ways, such as by assignments, projects and real-life case studies.

- You need to demonstrate specific knowledge and skills to achieve the learning outcomes set by Edexcel. You must achieve all the grading criteria to pass a unit.

- The grading criteria for pass, merit and distinction are shown in a grading grid for the unit. Higher-level skills are needed for higher grades.

- The assessment grades of pass, merit and distinction convert to unit points. The total unit points you receive for the course determines your final overall grade(s) and UCAS points.

TOP TIP

It's always tempting to spend longer on work you like doing and are good at, but focusing on improving your weak areas will do more to boost your overall grade(s).

Action points

1 Find out more about your own course by carrying out this activity.

a) Find the learning outcomes for the units you are currently studying. Your tutor may have given you these, or you can find them in your course specification – go to www.edexcel.com and search for your qualification.

b) Look at the grading grid for the units and identify the way the requirements change for the higher grades. If there are some unfamiliar words, check these in Step Six of this guide (see page 35 onwards).

c) If the unit points system still seems complicated, ask your tutor to explain it.

d) Check the UCAS points you would need for the course or university which interests you.

e) Design a form you can use to record the unit points you earn throughout your course. Keep this up-to-date. Regularly check how your points relate to your overall grade(s), based on the grade boundaries for your qualification. Your tutor can give you this information or you can check it yourself in the course specification.

Activity: UCAS Points

For each unit on the course, copy and complete the following table. Keep the tables in your BTEC file. This will help you to track your progress on the course to ensure you are on track to get the necessary UCAS points to go on to your chosen university degree or career.

A pass converts into 3 UCAS points, a merit converts into 6 UCAS points and a distinction converts into 12 UCAS points.

Unit number	Assignment number and title	Grade achieved	Conversion to UCAS points
		Overall grade	Total UCAS points

TOP TIP

Remember, many universities require at least a merit or 240 UCAS points overall to allow you on to a science-related degree course. Some may require a distinction or 360 UCAS points. Make sure you check what you will need early on in your course.

Step Three: Understand yourself

Case study: Being self-aware

Ben is studying on the BTEC Level 3 National Diploma in Applied Science (Medical Science). On completing his course, he wants to go to university to study Genetics and hopes, one day, to work as a genetic councillor at the Sanger Centre where the DNA code was unravelled.

Ben needs to start thinking about his own personality; he completes an online personality test to help him think about the skills and abilities that he has gained both before and during his course so far. This information will help him to complete a personal statement for his UCAS form when he applies to university.

Ben makes a brief list of his strengths which he can add to as the course proceeds. He can also refer back to the list in the future when he completes his personal statement. Ben tries to relate his list to the skills and abilities he thinks a genetic councillor needs.

'I have the following skills and abilities:

- I work well with other people and as part of a team.
- I am very creative and have prepared a leaflet for the public.
- I work very well under pressure and have handed in all my work to strict deadlines.
- I am extremely motivated to succeed in my studies both now and in the future.
- I am a very good communicator, both written and orally.
- I have a lot of empathy, am a good listener and am very tactful.'

Reflection points

Think about how you behave in a classroom situation:

- What do you think is your main strength?
- How can you put this strength to good use?
- What weakness(es) do you have?
- How can improve on your weaker areas?

Self-awareness means understanding how you 'tick'. For example, do you prefer practical activities rather than theory? Do you prefer to draw or sketch an idea, rather than write about it?

Self-awareness is important as it makes you less reliant on other people's opinions and gives you confidence in your own judgement. You can also reflect on your actions to learn from your experiences.

Self-awareness also means knowing your own strengths and weaknesses. Knowing your strengths enables you to feel positive and confident about yourself and your abilities. Knowing your weaknesses means you know the areas you need to develop.

You can analyse yourself by looking at...

... your personality and preferences

You may have taken a personality test at your centre. If not, your tutor may recommend one to use, or there are many available online.

Many employers ask job candidates to complete a personality test so that they can match the type of work they are offering to the most suitable candidates. Although these tests can only give a broad indication of someone's personality they may help to avoid mismatches, such as hiring someone who is introverted to work in sales.

... your skills and abilities

To succeed in your assignments, and to progress in a career, requires a number of skills. Some may be vocationally-specific, or professional, skills that you can improve during your course – such as sporting performance on a Sports course. Others are broader skills that are invaluable no matter what you are studying – such as communicating clearly and cooperating with others.

You will work faster and more accurately, and have greater confidence, if you are skilled and proficient. A quick skills check will identify any problem areas.

TOP TIP

Use the Skills Building section on page 93 to identify the skills you need for your course. You'll also find hints and tips for improving any weak areas.

Key points

- You need certain skills and abilities to get the most out of your BTEC Level 3 National course and to develop your career potential.
- Knowing your strengths and weaknesses is a sign of maturity. It gives you greater confidence in your abilities and enables you to focus on areas for improvement.

TOP TIP

You will find more help on developing your skills and abilities in the sections on: Working as a member of a group; Using time wisely; Researching and analysing information; and Making effective presentations.

Action points

1 Gain insight into your own personality by answering each of the following statements **True** or **False** with a tick. Be honest!

		True	False
a)	If someone annoys me, I can tell them about it without causing offence.		
b)	If someone is talking, I often interrupt them to give them my opinion.		
c)	I get really stressed if I'm under pressure.		
d)	I can sometimes become very emotional and upset on other people's behalf.		
e)	I sometimes worry that I can't cope and may make a mess of something.		
f)	I am usually keen, enthusiastic and motivated to do well.		
g)	I enjoy planning and organising my work.		
h)	I find it easy to work and cooperate with other people and take account of their opinions.		
i)	I am easily influenced by other people.		
j)	I often jump to conclusions and judge people and situations on first impressions.		
k)	I prefer to rely on facts and experience rather than following my instincts.		

Now identify which of the skills and qualities in the box below will be really important in your chosen career.

> tact   truthfulness   listening skills
>
> staying calm under pressure
>
> empathy with others   self-confidence
>
> initiative   planning and organising
>
> working with others   self-assurance
>
> objective judgements

Use your answers to identify areas you should work on to be successful in the future.

2 As part of the UCAS process, all **higher education** applicants have to write a personal statement. This is different from a CV, which is a summary of achievements that all job applicants prepare. You may have already prepared a CV but not thought about a personal statement. Now is your chance to!

Read the information about personal statements in the box. Then answer these questions:

a) Explain why personal statements are so important for higher education applicants.

b) Why do you think it is important for your personal statement to read well and be error-free?

c) Suggest three reasons why you shouldn't copy a pre-written statement you have found online.

d) Check the websites you can access from the hotlink given in the box to see what to include in the statement and how to set it out.

e) Prepare a bullet point list of ten personal facts. Focus on your strengths and good reasons why you should be given a place on the higher education course of your choice. If possible, discuss your list with your tutor. Then keep it safely, as it will be useful if you need to write a personal statement later.

Personal statements

This is the information that all higher education applicants have to put in the blank space on their UCAS form. The aim is to sell yourself to admissions tutors. It can be pretty scary, especially if you haven't written anything like it before.

So, where do you start?

First, *never* copy pre-written statements you find online. These are just for guidance. Even worse are websites that offer to write your statement for a fee, and send you a few general, pre-written paragraphs. Forget them all: you can do better!

Imagine you are an admissions tutor with 60 places to offer to 200 applicants. What will you need to read in a personal statement to persuade you to offer the applicant a place?

Most likely, clear explanations about:

- what the applicant can contribute to the course
- why the applicant really wants a place on your course
- what the applicant has done to further his or her own interests in this area, eg voluntary work
- attributes that show this applicant would be a definite bonus – such as innovative ideas, with evidence, eg 'I organised a newsletter which we published every three months …'

A personal statement should be well written, with no grammatical or spelling errors and organised into clear paragraphs.

There are a number of helpful websites with further information on personal statements. Go to page 104 to see how to access these websites.

Activity: Preparing your personal statement

Throughout the BTEC National in Applied Science course you will gain a lot of strengths in scientific practice. You will also identify areas of weakness and develop these into strengths.

When applying to university, you need to prepare a personal statement focusing on these strengths in a science-related context. It is a good idea to do this at the start of the course so that you have the information ready to complete your personal statement quickly and efficiently. It will also help you to address your weaknesses as you go along.

Some examples are given below. Write in some of your own in the space provided. Look at which strengths you will gain from completing the assessments during the course.

Strengths	Evidence
I can…	
• prepare a scientific report	I wrote up an investigation into the effect of temperature on enzyme activity.
• prepare and present a presentation	I prepared and delivered a PowerPoint presentation to the class on 'Genetic engineering' and gained a distinction grade.
• understand the day-to-day work of sports physiotherapists and the injuries they treat	I gained a distinction for the work experience assignment I did following a placement with a sports physiotherapist at Sheffield Wednesday football club.
• work safely and effectively in a laboratory	I investigated the effectiveness of different antibiotics to kill bacteria. I gained full marks for health and safety during the task.
•	
•	

TOP TIP

Create an electronic copy of the template above so you can update regularly your records on your strengths. Keep a paper copy of it in your file for future reference.

Step Four: Use your time wisely

Case study: Getting the balance right

Amy and Delroy are friends studying on the BTEC National in Applied Science (Forensic Science) course. Amy wants to work for the police as a forensic scientist and Delroy would like to go to university to study to become a molecular biologist. They both have different attitudes to completing work.

Amy is very good at organising her time and planning her work. She has made a diary to record when her assignments are due in, and plans small chunks of time when she can fit in her studies. She identifies in advance any resources she may need to collect for her assignments. Amy also makes a note of any commitments which may interfere with completing her assignments on time. She knows exactly what has to be done and by when, and always asks her tutor if she is unsure of anything. Although Amy is very conscientious, she also allows time for a social life.

Delroy is very different to Amy. He can't be bothered to make a diary and is used to completing his work at the last minute. He hopes to get all his work done at his centre; he has such a busy social life that he has no time to study. He is a member of a football team, loves spending time with his girlfriend and other friends. He is always listening to his ipod or on Facebook chatting to friends. Delroy has no real idea when he needs to hand in his assignments, but he can just ask Amy if he needs to know anything as she is really organised.

Reflection points

How organised are you?

Do you think there is anything you could do to improve your organisation?

Most learners have to combine course commitments with other responsibilities such as a job (either full- or part-time) and family responsibilities. You will also want to see your friends and keep up your hobbies and interests. Juggling these successfully means you need to be able to use your time wisely.

This involves planning what to do and when to do it to prevent panics about unexpected deadlines. As your course progresses, this becomes even more important as your workload may increase towards the end of a term. In some cases there could be two or more assignments to complete simultaneously. Although tutors try to avoid clashes of this sort, it is sometimes inevitable.

To cope successfully, you need time-management skills, in particular:

- how to organise your time to be more productive
- how to prioritise tasks
- how to overcome time-wasters.

Organising your time

- **Use a diary or wall chart.**
  Using a different colour pen for each, enter:
  - your course commitments, eg assignment dates, tutorials, visits
  - important personal commitments, eg sports matches, family birthdays
  - your work commitments.

TOP TIP

A diary is useful because you can update it as you go, but a wall chart gives you a better overview of your commitments over several weeks. Keep your diary or chart up to date and check ahead regularly so that you have prior warning of important dates.

- **Identify how you currently use your time.**
  - Work out how much time you spend at your centre, at work, at home and on social activities.
  - Identify which commitments are vital and which are optional so you can find extra time if necessary.

- **Plan and schedule future commitments.**
  - Write down any appointments and tasks you must do.
  - Enter assignment review dates and final deadline dates in different colours.
  - This should stop you from arranging a dental appointment on the same morning that you are due to give an important presentation – or planning a hectic social life when you have lots of course work to do.

- **Decide your best times for doing course work.**
  - Expect to do most of your course work in your own time.
  - Work at the time of day when you feel at your best.
  - Work regularly, and in relatively short bursts, rather than once or twice a week for very long stretches.
  - If you're a night owl, allow an hour to 'switch off' before you go to bed.

- **Decide where to work.**
  - Choose somewhere you can concentrate without interruption.
  - Make sure there is space for resources you use, such as books or specialist equipment.
  - You also need good lighting and a good – but not too comfortable – chair.
  - If you can't find suitable space at home, check out your local or college library.

- **Assemble the items you need.**
  - Book ahead to get specific books, journals or DVDs from the library.
  - Ensure you have your notes, handouts and assignment brief with you.
  - Use sticky notes to mark important pages in textbooks or folders.

TOP TIP

Set yourself a target when you start work, so that you feel positive and productive at the end. Always try to end a session when a task is going well, rather than when you are stuck. Then you will be keener to go back to it the next day. Note down outstanding tasks you need to continue with next time.

- **Plan ahead.**
  - If anything is unclear about an assignment, ask your tutor for an explanation as soon as you can.
  - Break down long tasks or assignments into manageable chunks, eg find information, decide what to use, create a plan for finished work, write rough draft of first section, etc.
  - Work back from deadline dates so that you allow plenty of time to do the work.
  - Always allow more time than you need. It is better to finish early than to run out of time.

TOP TIP

If you are working on a task as a group, organise and agree times to work together. Make sure you have somewhere to meet where you can work without disturbing other courses or groups.

- **Be self-disciplined.**
  - Don't put things off because you're not in the mood. Make it easier by doing simple tasks first to get a sense of achievement. Then move on to something harder.
  - Plan regular breaks. If you're working hard you need a change of activity to recharge your batteries.
  - If you have a serious problem or personal crisis, talk to your personal tutor promptly.

TOP TIP

Make sure you know the consequences of missing an assignment deadline, as well as the dispensations and exemptions that can be given if you have an unavoidable and serious problem, such as illness (see also page 90).

How to prioritise tasks

Prioritising means doing the most important and urgent task first. Normally this will be the task or assignment with the closest deadline or the one that will most affect your overall course grades.

One way of prioritising is to group tasks into ABC categories.

Category A tasks	These must be done now as they are very important and cannot be delayed, eg completing an assignment to be handed in tomorrow.
Category B tasks	These are jobs you should do if you have time, because otherwise they will rapidly become Category A, eg getting a book that you need for your next assignment.
Category C tasks	These are tasks you should do if you have the time, eg rewriting notes jotted down quickly in a lesson.

Expect to be flexible. For example, if you need to allow time for information to arrive, then send for this first. If you are working in a team, take into account other people's schedules when you are making arrangements.

Avoiding time-wasters

Everyone has days when they don't know where the time has gone. It may be because they were constantly interrupted or because things just kept going wrong. Whatever the reason, the end result is that some jobs don't get done.

If this happens to you regularly, you need to take steps to keep on track.

Some useful tips are:

- **Warn people in advance when you will be working.**
  - Ask them to not interrupt you.
  - If you are in a separate room, shut the door. If someone comes in, make it clear you don't want to talk.
  - If that doesn't work, find somewhere else (or some other time) to work.
- **Switch off your mobile, TV, radio and iPod/MP3 player.**
  - Don't respond to, or make, calls or texts.
  - If someone rings your home phone, let voicemail answer or ask them to call back later.
- **Be strict with yourself when you are working online.**
  - Don't check your email until you've finished work.
  - Don't get distracted when searching for information.
  - Keep away from social networking sites.
- **Avoid displacement activities.**
  - These are the normally tedious jobs, such as cleaning your computer screen, that suddenly seem far more attractive than working!

Talking to friends can occupy a lot of time.

TOP TIP

The first step in managing your own time is learning to say 'no' (nicely!) if someone asks you to do something tempting when you should be working.

Key points

- Being in control of your time allows you to balance your commitments according to their importance and means you won't let anyone down.
- Organising yourself and your time involves knowing how you spend your time now, planning when and where it is best to work, scheduling commitments and setting sensible timescales to complete your work.
- Knowing how to prioritise means you will schedule work effectively according to its urgency and importance. You will need self-discipline to follow the schedule you have set for yourself.
- Identifying ways in which you may waste time means you can guard against these to achieve your goals more easily.

TOP TIP

Benefits to managing your own time include being less stressed (because you are not reacting to problems or crises), producing better work and having time for a social life.

Action points

1 Start planning your time properly.

a) Find out how many assignments you will have this term, and when you will get them. Put this information into your diary or planner.

b) Update this with your other commitments for the term – both work/course-related and social. Identify possible clashes and decide how to resolve the problem.

c) Identify one major task or assignment you will do soon. Divide it into manageable chunks and decide how long to allow for each chunk, plus some spare time for any problems. If possible, check your ideas with your tutor before you put them into your planner.

2 How good are you at being responsible for your own learning?

a) Fill in the following table. Score yourself out of 5 for each area: where 0 is awful and 5 is excellent. Ask a friend or relative to score you as well. See if you can explain any differences.

	Scoring yourself	Other person's score for you
Being punctual		
Organisational ability		
Tidiness		
Working accurately		
Finding and correcting your mistakes		
Solving problems		
Accepting responsibility		
Working with details		
Planning how to do a job		
Using your initiative		
Thinking up new ideas		
Meeting deadlines		

b) Draw up your own action plan for areas where you need to improve. If possible, talk this through at your next **tutorial**.

TOP TIP

Don't waste time doing things that distract you when studying for this course. In all industries, time costs money.

Activity: Managing your time

Complete the table below and update it during your course. This will help you to think about how you can manage your time well on your BTEC National course. Planning ahead will help you to complete your assignments on time and to the best of your ability, avoiding problems and stress. An example has been added to help you.

Assignment number Title Tutor	First hand-in date	Re-submission date	Times and dates to work on this assignment	Commitments/problems that may interfere with this assignment
Unit 3.1 The Nervous System JM	20th Sept	14th Oct	Monday – Friday 5–7pm starting on 6.9.10	My birthday Thursday Weekend away next Friday Need to get books from library

Step Five: Utilise all your resources

Case study: Using your resources

Sadaf really wants to become a radiologist. She hopes to study Radiotherapy at university on completion of her BTEC National Diploma in Applied Science (Medical Science). She needs to get at least an overall merit at the end of the BTEC National to be accepted onto the university course. She is an excellent learner, works really hard and tries to get distinctions in her units.

She has been given an assignment brief on 'Reproduction and In-vitro Fertilisation (IVF)'. Sadaf is really interested in this particular assignment as the work of a radiologist can involve scanning women who are undergoing assisted conception as part of the IVF process, and scanning pregnant women.

The grading criteria for the assignment are set out in three sections with tasks for pass, merit and distinction. Sadaf decides to make some notes of the general resources she will use to complete this assignment. Before she starts, she makes sure she has found everything she requires, ticking each one off as she goes.

'I need:

- handouts from my tutor on reproduction and IVF
- my personal notes from the lesson
- a study buddy to make notes for me, collect handouts and other information if I am ever absent (get telephone number and email address)
- a pen, pencil, paper, ruler, calculator
- a file with coloured dividers to keep handouts and information for each unit in separate sections
- useful websites on reproduction and IVF treatment (research on the internet)
- useful books on reproduction and IVF treatment (go to the library)
- telephone numbers for IVF clinics.'

Reflection points

Think about the materials and equipment you will need when you start the course. Make a list.

Have you got somewhere quiet to work when you are not at college?

Your resources are all the things that can help you to be successful in your BTEC Level 3 National qualification, from your favourite website to your **study buddy** (see page 32) who collects handouts for you if you miss a class.

Your centre will provide essential resources, such as a library with appropriate books and electronic reference sources, the computer network and internet access. You will have to provide basic resources such as pens, pencils and file folders yourself. If you have to buy your own textbooks, look after them carefully so you can sell them on at the end of your course.

Here is a list of resources, with tips for getting the best out of them.

- **Course information**. This includes your course specification, this Study Skills Guide and all information on the Edexcel website relating to your BTEC Level 3 National course. Course information from your centre will include term dates, assignment dates and your timetable. Keep everything safely so you can refer to it whenever you need to clarify something.

- **Course materials**. These include course handouts, printouts, your own notes and textbooks. Put handouts into an A4 folder as soon as you get them. Use a separate folder for each unit you study.

TOP TIP

Filing notes and handouts promptly means they don't get lost, will stay clean and uncrumpled and you won't waste time looking for them.

- **Stationery**. You need pens and pencils, a notepad, a hole puncher, a stapler and sets of dividers. Dividers should be clearly labelled to help you store and quickly find notes, printouts and handouts. Your notes should be headed and dated, and those from your own research must also include your source (see Step Eight – page 71 onwards.)

- **People**. Your tutors, specialist staff at college, classmates, your employer and work colleagues, your relatives and friends are all valuable resources. Many will have particular skills or work in the vocational area that you are studying. Talking to other learners can help to clarify issues that there may not have been time to discuss fully in class.

A **study buddy** is another useful resource as they can make notes and collect handouts if you miss a session. (Remember to return the favour when they are away.)

Always be polite when you are asking people for information. Prepare the questions first and remember that you are asking for help, not trying to get them to do the work for you! If you are interviewing someone for an assignment or project, good preparations are vital. (See Step Eight – page 71 onwards.)

If someone who did the course before you offers help, be careful. It is likely the course requirements will have changed. Never be tempted to copy their assignments (or someone else's). This is **plagiarism** – a deadly sin in the educational world (see also Step Six – page 35.)

TOP TIP

A positive attitude, an enquiring mind and the ability to focus on what is important will have a major impact on your final result.

Key points

- Resources help you to achieve your qualification. Find out what resources you have available to you and use them wisely.
- Have your own stationery items.
- Know how to use central facilities and resources such as the library, learning resource centres and your computer network. Always keep to the policy on IT use in your centre.
- People are a key resource – school or college staff, work colleagues, members of your class, friends, family and people who are experts in their field.

Action points

1 a) List the resources you will need to complete your course successfully. Identify which ones will be provided by your school or college, and which you need to supply yourself.

b) Go through your list again and identify the resources you already have (or know how to access) and those you don't.

c) Compare your list with a friend's and decide how to obtain and access the resources you need. Add any items to your list that you forgot.

d) List the items you still need to get and set a target date for doing this.

2 'Study buddy' schemes operate in many centres. Find out if this applies to your own centre and how you can make the best use of it.

In some you can choose your study buddy, in others people are paired up by their tutor.
- Being a study buddy might mean just collecting handouts when the other person is absent, and giving them important news.
- It may also mean studying together and meeting (or keeping in contact by phone or email) to exchange ideas and share resources.

With a study buddy you can share resources and stay on top of the course if you're ever away.

Activity: Resources

Create an electronic copy of the template below to help you prepare for each assignment. When you are given an assignment, make a list of the things that you need to help you complete it to a distinction grade. Keep this safely in your file for future reference.

Assignment number	
Assignment title	
Things I need	**Resources**
stationery	
books (references with page numbers)	
websites (references)	
newspaper/TV articles (references)	
journals (references)	
expert advice (tutor/external agency/external speaker)	
study buddy	
handouts/printouts/my own notes (in file)	

TOP TIP

Listing the references for books, websites, journals, newspaper articles and TV programmes as you go along will make things easier for you. You can add references you have used to your assignment at the end. This will save lots of time looking for essential references later on.

Step Six: Understand your assessment

Case study: Gaining the marks you need

Arsalan has been given his first assignment on the BTEC Level 3 National Subsidiary Diploma in Applied Science course. He wants to be successful on this course to enable him to go on to university to study Biochemistry. He plans a future career as a biochemist.

First, Arsalan reads the assignment brief several times and makes sure that he understands the learning outcomes and grading criteria. He is a bit unsure about what some of the merit and distinction grading criteria mean, so he asks his tutor. He makes an early start and works on one section at a time. Arsalan uses his notes from the lessons to help him complete the pass criteria. He also spends time looking for and reading several books, journals and websites. This helps him to complete the merit and distinction criteria. He is selective in his use of information and leaves left out any that he thinks is irrelevant. However, some of the work that Arsalan does for the distinction criteria is a bit rushed; he didn't allow enough time at the end to complete it properly and check it through.

Arsalan hands in his assignment on time and the tutor gives him valuable feedback on how to improve his work: for the distinction criteria, Arsalan has made some silly mistakes and he also gave an 'explanation' instead of 'evaluating' a chemistry investigation. Arsalan realises that he made these mistakes because he rushed to finish his assignment. He amends and adds to the assignment as the tutor suggests, ending up with a distinction grade.

Reflection points

Do you know how to carry out effective research?

What is constructive criticism and how can it help you improve your grades?

Being successful on any BTEC Level 3 National course means first understanding what you must do in your assignments – and then doing it.

Your assignments focus on topics you have already covered in class. If you've attended regularly, you should be able to complete them confidently.

However, there are some common pitfalls it's worth thinking about. Here are tips to avoid them:

- Read the instructions (the assignment brief) properly and several times before you start.

- Make sure you understand what you are supposed to do. Ask if anything is unclear.

- Complete every part of a task. If you ignore a question, you can't meet the grading criteria.

- Prepare properly. Do your research or reading before you start. Don't guess the answers.

- Communicate your ideas clearly. You can check this by asking someone who doesn't know the subject to look at your work.

- Only include relevant information. Padding out answers makes it look as if you don't know your subject.

- Do the work earlier rather than later to avoid any last-minute panics.

- Pay attention to advice and feedback that your tutor has given you.

The assignment 'brief'

This may be longer than its name implies! The assignment brief includes all the instructions for an assignment and several other details, as you can see in the table below.

What will you find in a BTEC Level 3 National assignment brief?	
Content	**Details**
Title	This will link to the unit and learning outcomes
Format/style	Written assignment, presentation, demonstration, etc
Preparation	Read case study, do research, etc
Learning outcomes	These state the knowledge you must demonstrate to obtain a required grade
Grading criterion/ criteria covered	eg P1/M1/D1
Individual/group work	Remember to identify your own contribution in any group work
Feedback	Tutor, peer review
Interim review dates	Dates to see your tutor
Final deadline	Last submission date

Your centre's rules and regulations

Your centre will have several policies and guidelines about assignments, which you need to check carefully. Many, such as those listed below, relate to Edexcel policies and guidelines.

- The procedure to follow if you have a serious problem and can't meet a deadline. An extension may be granted.
- The penalty for missing a deadline without good reason.
- The penalty for copying someone else's work. This is usually severe, so never share your work (or CDs or USB flash drive) with anyone else, and don't borrow theirs.
- **Plagiarism** is also serious misconduct. This means copying someone's work (see also page 32) or quoting from books and websites and pretending it is your own work.
- The procedure to follow if you disagree with the grade you are given.

Understanding the question or task

There are two aspects to a question or task. The first is the **command words**, which are described on pages 37–39. The second is the **presentation instructions**, which is what you are asked to do – don't write a report when you should be producing a chart!

Command words, such as 'explain', 'describe', 'analyse' and 'evaluate' state how a question must be answered. You may be asked to 'describe' something at pass level, but you will need to do more, perhaps 'analyse' or 'evaluate', to achieve merit or distinction.

Many learners fail to achieve higher grades because they don't realise the difference between these words. Instead of analysing or evaluating they give an explanation instead. Adding more details won't achieve a higher grade – you need to change your whole approach to the answer.

The **grading grid** for each unit of your course gives you the command words, so that you know

what to do to achieve a pass, merit or distinction. The tables that follow show you what is usually required when you see a particular command word. These are just examples to guide you as the exact response will depend on the question. If you have any doubts, check with your tutor before you start work.

There are two important points to note.

- A command word, such as 'create' or 'explain' may be repeated in the grading criteria for different grades. In these cases the complexity or range of the task itself increases at the higher grades.
- Command words vary depending on your vocational area. So Art and Design grading grids may use different command words from Applied Science, for example.

TOP TIP

Look at this section again when you get your first assignment and check the command words against these explanations.

To obtain a pass grade

To achieve a pass you must usually demonstrate that you understand the important facts relating to a topic and can state these clearly and concisely.

Command words for a pass	Meaning
Create (or produce)	Make, invent or construct an item.
Describe	Give a clear, straightforward description that includes all the main points and links these together logically.
Define	Clearly explain what a particular term means and give an example, if appropriate, to show what you mean.
Explain … how/why	Set out in detail the meaning of something, with reasons. It is often helpful to give an example of what you mean. Start with the topic then give the 'how' or 'why'.
Identify	Distinguish and state the main features or basic facts relating to a topic.
Interpret	Define or explain the meaning of something.
Illustrate	Give examples to show what you mean.
List	Provide the information required in a list rather than in continuous writing.
Outline	Write a clear description that includes all the main points but avoid going into too much detail.
Plan (or devise)	Work out and explain how you would carry out a task or activity.
Select (and present) information	Identify relevant information to support the argument you are making and communicate this in an appropriate way.
State	Write a clear and full account.
Undertake	Carry out a specific activity.
Examples:	
Identify the main features on a digital camera.	
Outline the steps to take to carry out research for an assignment.	

To obtain a merit grade

To obtain a merit you must prove that you can
apply your knowledge in a specific way.

Command words for a merit	Meaning
Analyse	Identify separate factors, say how they relate to each other and how each one relates to the topic.
Classify	Sort your information into appropriate categories before presenting or explaining it.
Compare and contrast	Identify the main factors that apply in two or more situations and explain the similarities and differences or advantages and disadvantages.
Demonstrate	Provide several relevant examples or appropriate evidence which support the arguments you are making. In some vocational areas this may also mean giving a practical performance.
Discuss	Provide a thoughtful and logical argument to support the case you are making.
Explain (in detail)	Provide details and give reasons and/or evidence to clearly support the argument you are making.
Implement	Put into practice or operation. You may also have to interpret or justify the effect or result.
Interpret	Understand and explain an effect or result.
Justify	Give appropriate reasons to support your opinion or views and show how you arrived at these conclusions.
Relate/report	Give a full account, with reasons.
Research	Carry out a full investigation.
Specify	Provide full details and descriptions of selected items or activities.
Examples: Compare and contrast the performance of two different digital cameras. Explain in detail the steps to take to research an assignment.	

To obtain a distinction grade

To obtain a distinction you must prove that you can make a reasoned judgement based on appropriate evidence.

Command words for a distinction	Meaning
Analyse	Identify the key factors, show how they are linked and explain the importance and relevance of each.
Assess	Give careful consideration to all the factors or events that apply and identify which are the most important and relevant, with reasons.
Comprehensively explain	Give a very detailed explanation that covers all the relevant points and give reasons for your views or actions.
Critically comment	Give your view after you have considered all the evidence, particularly the importance of both the relevant positive and negative aspects.
Evaluate	Review the information and then bring it together to form a conclusion. Give evidence to support each of your views or statements.
Evaluate critically	Review the information to decide the degree to which something is true, important or valuable. Then assess possible alternatives, taking into account their strengths and weaknesses if they were applied instead. Then give a precise and detailed account to explain your opinion.
Summarise	Identify/review the main, relevant factors and/or arguments so that these are explained in a clear and concise manner.
Examples:	
Assess ten features commonly found on a digital camera.	
Analyse your own ability to carry out effective research for an assignment.	

TOP TIP

Check that you understand exactly how you need to demonstrate each of the learning outcomes specified in the assignment.

Responding positively

Assignments enable you to demonstrate what you know and how you can apply it. You should respond positively to the challenge and give it your best shot. Being well organised and having confidence in your own abilities helps too, and this is covered in the next section.

Key points

- Read instructions carefully so that you don't make mistakes that can easily be avoided, such as only doing part of the set task.
- Note the assignment deadline on your planner and any interim review dates. Schedule work around these dates to make the most of reviews with your tutor.
- Check your centre's policies relating to assignments, such as how to obtain an extension or query a final grade.
- Expect command words and/or the complexity of a task to be different at higher grades, because you have to demonstrate higher-level skills.

TOP TIP

All your assignments will relate to topics you have covered and work you have done in class. They're not meant to be a test to catch you out.

Action points

1 Check your ability to differentiate between different types of command words by doing this activity.
   a) Prepare a brief description of your usual lifestyle (pass level).
   b) Describe and justify your current lifestyle (merit level).
   c) Critically evaluate your current lifestyle (distinction level).

It would be a good idea to check that your answer is accurate and appropriate by showing it to your tutor at your next tutorial.

TOP TIP

When presenting evidence for an assessment, think about the person who will be looking through it. Plan your 'pitch' well and make it easy for the assessor to match your evidence against the grading criteria.

Sample assignment

Note about assignments

All learners are different and will approach their assignments in different ways. The sample assignment that follows shows how one learner answered a brief to achieve pass, merit and distinction level criteria. The learner's work shows just one way in which these grading criteria can be evidenced. There are no standard or set answers. If you produce the required evidence for each task then you will achieve the grading criteria covered by the assignment.

Sample assignment front sheet

Complete the front sheet before submitting work. Add your name, signature and the date.

Ensure work is handed in for the final deadline. Your centre will have rules for you to follow on this.

Ask your tutor for feedback on the work you have completed before you submit it.

This front sheet must be completed by the learner where appropriate and included with the work submitted for assessment.

Learner name		Assessor name
Jason Evans		Mr J Morris

Date issued	Completion date		Submitted on
10 November 2010	10 December 2010		9 December 2010

Qualification		Unit
BTEC Level 3 National Diploma in Applied Science		Unit 1: Fundamentals of Science

Assignment title	Atomic structure, the periodic table, bonding and titrations

In this assessment you will have opportunities to provide evidence against the following criteria. Indicate the page numbers where the evidence can be found.

Criteria reference	To achieve the criteria the evidence must show that the learner is able to:	Task no.	Page numbers
P1	outline the key features of the periodic table, atomic structure and chemical bonding	1	1–7
P2	demonstrate practically the ability to prepare chemical solutions and test their accuracy	2	8–10
M1	relate the key features of the periodic table to the conclusions drawn from the practical activities	3	11
D1	explain how standard solutions and titrations are prepared in industry	4	12–19

Learner declaration
I certify that the work submitted for this assignment is my own and research sources are fully acknowledged.

Learner signature: *Jason Evans*   Date: *9 December 2010*

It is extremely important that you meet the criteria in this table in a way that provides specific evidence to satisfy the assessment process.

Remember that plagiarism is not acceptable. Use your centre's chosen method to reference all copied phrases, illustrations and text.

You must provide specific evidence based on the criteria for this particular assignment. The brief will guide you on possible different ways to provide this evidence.

Sample assignment brief

The scenario explains the context of the assignment – in this case it asks you to assume the role of a science practitioner.

Unit title	Unit 1: Fundamentals of Science
Qualification	BTEC Level 3 National Diploma in Applied Science
Start date	10 November 2010
Deadline date	10 December 2010
Assessor	Mr J Morris

Assignment title	Atomic structure, the periodic table, bonding and titrations

The purpose of this assignment is to:
allow you to demonstrate your knowledge, skills and understanding of some fundamental concepts in chemistry.

Scenario
You are a new technician working for Chemsol, a chemical company. Chemsol has been approached by Edvisprog, a company that produces visual aids and teaching resources for education. Edvisprog is planning a series of worksheets, handouts and videos of practicals for a web-based set of teaching and learning resources on the use of titrations. The senior technician at Chemsol has asked you to help create a portfolio of material for Edvisprog. Some of this material will draw on worksheets in Chemsol's testing and induction pack.

Task 1
It is planned to include several worksheets in Edvisprog's teaching and learning resource pack. You need to work through and complete some worksheets so that Edvisprog can supply teachers with the correct answers. You have been given five worksheets to complete (see attachment to this brief).

Worksheet 1:   Atomic structure

Worksheet 2:   The electronic structure, atomic number and mass number of the first twenty elements

Worksheet 3:   The electronic structures of the first twenty elements

Worksheet 4:   The periodic table

Worksheet 5:   Bonding

This provides evidence for P1

Task 2
You must now undertake some practical work which can be recorded for a video for the web-based resource. (In practice, your tutor will observe you completing the practical work in the task.)

The details of the practicals are set out in two worksheets (again provided with this brief). You must conduct the experiments described and complete the necessary calculations as set out in the worksheets.

Worksheet 6:   Preparation of a standard solution of sodium carbonate

Worksheet 7:   Titration to determine the equation for the reaction between hydrochloric acid and sodium carbonate

This provides evidence for P2

Keep referring back to the assignment tasks and grading criteria to ensure you are on the right track.

A standard solution describes a solution of a known concentration and is normally used in titrations.

It is essential to have a copy of the periodic table to help you to complete all the criteria required for Task 1.

Conclusions are the judgements that you make following the practical investigation. You should link your findings to current scientific information.

Titration involves adding a known volume of a solution of known concentration to a measured amount of a solution of unknown concentration until the reaction is complete. The result can then be calculated.

Task 3

In order to consolidate the material presented in the worksheets and practicals, Edvisprog will be publishing some supporting documentation. You have been asked to draft one of these documents. You need to explain how key features of the periodic table relate to the conclusions drawn from the practical work.

This provides evidence for M1

Task 4

It is important that people using the Edvisprog material understand the relevance and importance of titration for industry. So for this final task, you need to draft a further document for the education pack. In this document, you should explain and illustrate how standard solutions are prepared and titrations carried out in industry. Give information on the various methods of carrying out titrations in an industrial environment.

This provides evidence for D1

Sources of information

Websites

A visual interpretation of the table of elements
www.rsc.org/chemsoc/visualelements/index.htm

This brief has been verified as being fit for purpose			
Assessor	Mr J Morris		
Signature	J Morris	Date	11 October 2010
Internal verifier	Ms A Cooke		
Signature	Angela Cooke	Date	11 October 2010

Use sources of information that have been carefully chosen to allow you to complete the assignment effectively.

Sample learner work

All questions have been completed correctly. In this case, a single word answer for each question was adequate to fulfil the criteria for P1.

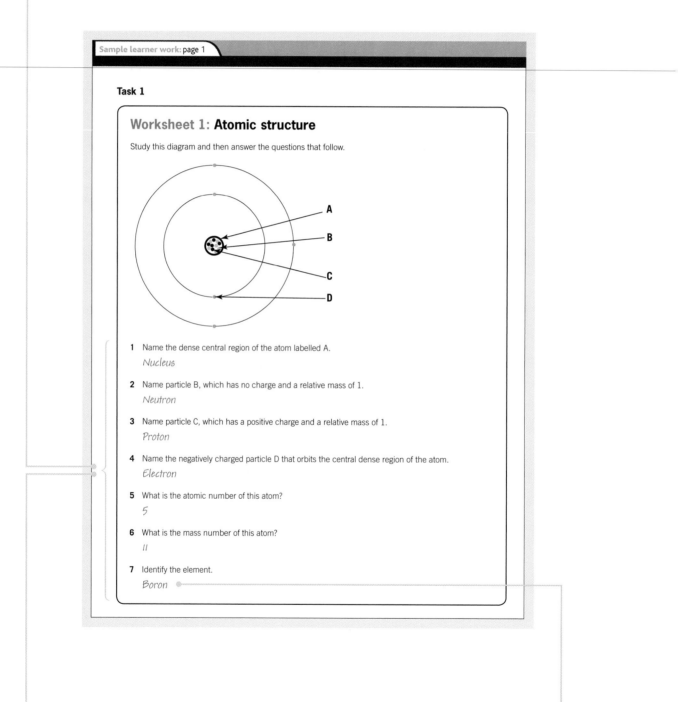

Sample learner work: page 1

Task 1

Worksheet 1: Atomic structure

Study this diagram and then answer the questions that follow.

1   Name the dense central region of the atom labelled A.
Nucleus

2   Name particle B, which has no charge and a relative mass of 1.
Neutron

3   Name particle C, which has a positive charge and a relative mass of 1.
Proton

4   Name the negatively charged particle D that orbits the central dense region of the atom.
Electron

5   What is the atomic number of this atom?
5

6   What is the mass number of this atom?
11

7   Identify the element.
Boron

The learner has used the correct spellings for scientific words.

A periodic table will help you to identify unknown atoms and to complete the questions, contributing to the P1 criterion.

> The learner has presented the correct numerical data to complete the worksheet as further evidence for P1.

Worksheet 2: The electronic structure, atomic number and mass number of the first twenty elements

Complete this table, which relates to the electronic structure, atomic numbers and mass numbers of the first twenty elements.

Element	Symbol	Number of protons	Number of neutrons	Atomic number	Mass number	Number of electrons	Electronic structure (orbitals)						Electronic structure (shells)
							1s	2s	2p	3s	3p	4s	
Hydrogen	H	1	0	1	1	1	1						1
Helium	He	2	2	2	4	2	2						2
Lithium	Li	3	4	3	7	3	2	1					2.1
Beryllium	Be	4	5	4	9	4	2	2					2.2
Boron	B	5	6	5	11	5	2	2	1				2.3
Carbon	C	6	6	6	12	6	2	2	2				2.4
Nitrogen	N	7	7	7	14	7	2	2	3				2.5
Oxygen	O	8	8	8	16	8	2	2	4				2.6
Fluorine	F	9	10	9	19	9	2	2	5				2.7
Neon	Ne	10	10	10	20	10	2	2	6				2.8
Sodium	Na	11	12	11	23	11	2	2	6	1			2.8.1
Magnesium	Mg	12	12	12	24	12	2	2	6	2			2.8.2
Aluminium	Al	13	14	13	27	13	2	2	6	2	1		2.8.3
Silicon	Si	14	14	14	28	14	2	2	6	2	2		2.8.4
Phosphorus	P	15	16	15	31	15	2	2	6	2	3		2.8.5
Sulphur	S	16	16	16	32	16	2	2	6	2	4		2.8.6
Chlorine	Cl	17	18	17	35	17	2	2	6	2	5		2.8.7
Argon	Ar	18	22	18	40	18	2	2	6	2	6		2.8.8
Potassium	K	19	20	19	39	19	2	2	6	2	6	1	2.8.8.1
Calcium	Ca	20	20	20	40	20	2	2	6	2	6	2	2.8.8.2

All the electronic structures have been drawn correctly on the shell of each atom.

Worksheet 3: The electronic structures of the first twenty elements

Complete the electronic structures of the first twenty elements, using crosses to represent electrons.

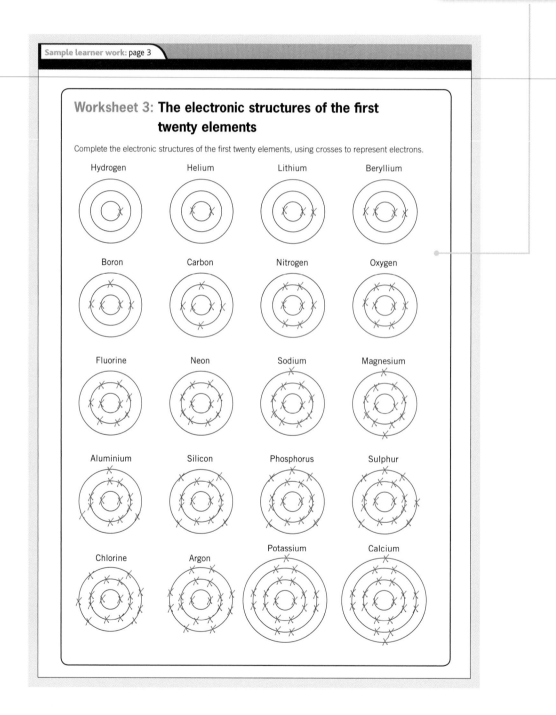

Sample learner work: page 4

Worksheet 4: The periodic table

Answer these questions on the periodic table.

1   What names are given to the vertical columns and horizontal rows in the periodic table?

   Vertical columns   *Groups*

   Horizontal rows   *Period*

2   Complete this table.

Element	Atomic number	Period	Group	Metal or non-metal?	Block (s, p or d)
Boron	5	2	3	Non Metal	p
Oxygen	8	2	6	Non Metal	p
Sodium	11	3	1	Metal	s
Aluminium	13	3	3	Metal	p
Phosphorus	15	3	5	Non Metal	p
Iron	26	4		Metal	d

3   a)   State what happens to the melting points of the elements as a period is crossed.

   The melting point rises to around 4000° Kelvin but when it reaches Group 4 the melting point drops to 0° in Group 5 and stays this way across the rest of the period.

   b)   State what happens to the first ionisation energy of the elements as:

   i) a period is crossed: *it increases*

   ii) a group is descended: *it decreases*

   c)   State what happens to the atomic radii of the elements as:

   i) a period is crossed: *it decreases*

   ii) a group is descended: *it increases*

4   Consider these three elements: **magnesium (Mg), silicon (Si) and chlorine (Cl)**.

   a)   Place them in order of their melting points:

   Highest: *Si*   Middle: *Mg*   Lowest: *Cl*

   b)   Place then in order of their first ionisation energies:

   Highest: *Cl*   Middle: *Si*   Lowest: *Mg*

   c)   Place them in order of their atomic radii:

   Largest: *Mg*   Middle: *Si*   Smallest: *Cl*

Worksheet 4: continued...

5 Consider these three elements: **lithium (Li), sodium (Na) and potassium (K)**

   a) Place then in order of their first ionisation energies:

      Highest: *Li*   Middle: *Na*   Lowest: *K*

   b) Place them in order of their atomic radii:

      Largest: *K*   Middle: *Na*   Smallest: *Li*

6 a) Predict which **two** of the elements listed below are **most likely** to show chemical reactions similar to those of chlorine.

argon	bromine	calcium
iodine	magnesium	phosphorus
potassium	rubidium	silicon
strontium	sulphur	

    Elements showing similar chemical reactions to chlorine: *bromine, iodine*

   b) Which element of the two that you have given as your answer to 6 a) is likely to be the most reactive with water?

    bromine

   c) From the list of elements given in question 6 a), select **two** elements that:

    i) produce basic oxides upon reaction with oxygen:

    magnesium   calcium

    ii) produce acidic solutions upon reaction with water (argon, phosphorus and sulphur don't react with water):

    silicon   iodine

An example of good practice, the work is presented correctly and neatly using a pencil and ruler.

Worksheet 5: **Bonding**

1   Complete these sentences by filling in the missing words.

Ionic compounds are formed by the *transfer* of electrons between atoms.

Metals form *positively* charged ions by *losing* electrons whereas non-metals form n*egatively* charged ions by *gaining* electrons.

Oppositely charged ions attract each other *electrostatically*. The ions form giant regular *lattice* structures in which *several* oppositely charged ions attract each other.

Covalent compounds are usually formed between *non-metals*.

They are formed by the *sharing* of a *pair* of electrons.

Each atom in a covalent bond contributes (a number) *one* electron(s) to the bond.

In both types of bonding the atoms of the elements become more stable by achieving the same electronic configuration as a *noble gas*.

2   Complete the table by listing the type of bonding in each substances.

Substance	Type of bonding
NaF	*Ionic*
MgO	*Ionic*
CCl4	*Covalent*
SO2	*Covalent*
CaS	*Ionic*
Cl2	*Chlorine*

3   **a)**   Identify the type of bonding in KF.

Ionic

   b)   Complete this dot and cross diagram for KF, showing only the outer electron shells.

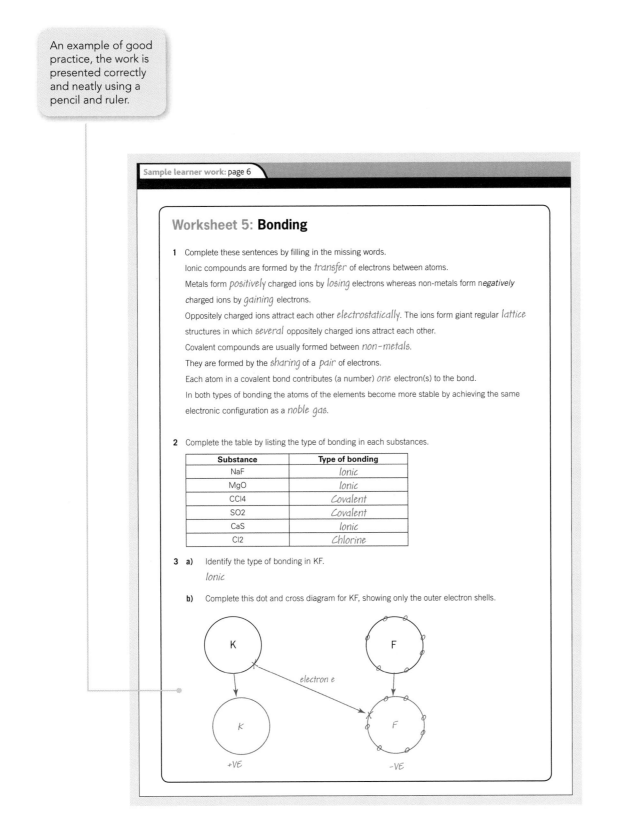

The learner has used the appropriate equipment (a protractor, compass, pencil and ruler) to present this work correctly and neatly. It is the final piece of evidence for successful completion of P1.

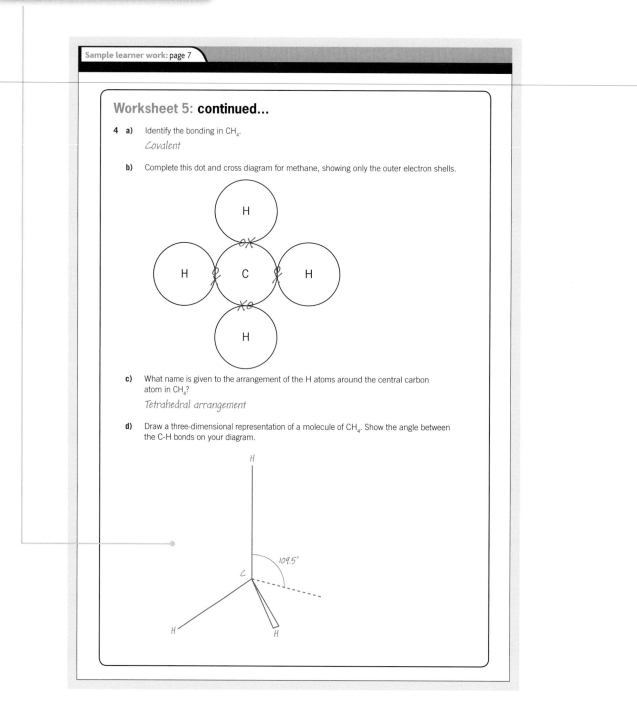

Worksheet 5: continued...

4 a) Identify the bonding in CH_4.

Covalent

b) Complete this dot and cross diagram for methane, showing only the outer electron shells.

c) What name is given to the arrangement of the H atoms around the central carbon atom in CH_4?

Tetrahedral arrangement

d) Draw a three-dimensional representation of a molecule of CH_4. Show the angle between the C-H bonds on your diagram.

109.5°

For P2, the learner has correctly completed the table, adding the relevant units and putting the decimal point in the correct place.

Task 2

Worksheet 6: Preparation of a standard solution of sodium carbonate

Procedure

Weigh an empty weighing boat and record its mass in the table (see readings below).

Add about 1.5 g sodium carbonate to the boat and record the mass accurately.

Transfer the sodium carbonate to a beaker and reweigh the boat recording its mass in the table.

Add about 100 cm³ of distilled water to the beaker containing the sodium carbonate and stir to dissolve.

Transfer the solution to the 250 cm³ volumetric flask using a funnel, washing down the stirring rod with a small amount of distilled water from a wash bottle. Rinse the beaker into the funnel again using distilled water from the wash bottle, and finally rinse the funnel and remove it before making up to the mark on the volumetric flask with distilled water. Add the last few drops of distilled water with a pastette (transfer pipette).

Readings

Mass of weighing boat in grams	2.210 g
Mass of weighing boat + Na_2CO_3 in grams	3.706 g
Mass of weighing boat + residual Na_2CO_3 in grams	2.221 g

Calculations

Mass of Na_2CO_3 in grams	$= 3.706 - 2.221 = 1.485$ g
M_r of Na_2CO_3	$= (23 \times 2) + 12 + (16 \times 3) = 46 + 12 + 48 = 106$
Moles of Na_2CO_3	$= 1.485 / 106 = 0.014$
Volume	$= 250 / 1000 = 0.25$
Concentration of Na_2CO_3 in mol dm⁻³	$= 0.014 / 0.25 = 0.0560$ mol dm⁻³

The learner has given the correct units where relevant for each calculation. You may need to look up some units if you are unsure which ones to use.

It is good practice to show workings for the assessor to mark.

It is good practice to collate all the materials and apparatus before you start any investigation.

Always follow health and safety guidelines when carrying out practical work.

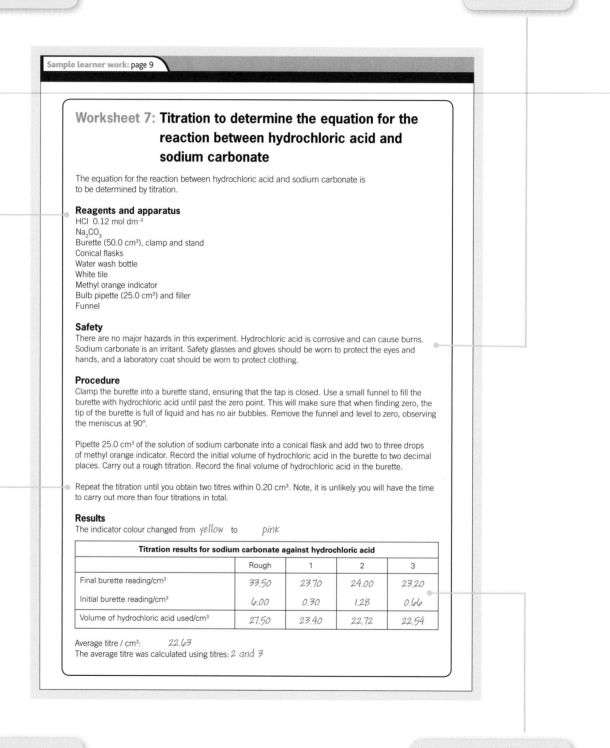

Sample learner work: page 9

Worksheet 7: Titration to determine the equation for the reaction between hydrochloric acid and sodium carbonate

The equation for the reaction between hydrochloric acid and sodium carbonate is to be determined by titration.

Reagents and apparatus
HCl 0.12 mol dm^{-3}
Na_2CO_3
Burette (50.0 cm^3), clamp and stand
Conical flasks
Water wash bottle
White tile
Methyl orange indicator
Bulb pipette (25.0 cm^3) and filler
Funnel

Safety
There are no major hazards in this experiment. Hydrochloric acid is corrosive and can cause burns. Sodium carbonate is an irritant. Safety glasses and gloves should be worn to protect the eyes and hands, and a laboratory coat should be worn to protect clothing.

Procedure
Clamp the burette into a burette stand, ensuring that the tap is closed. Use a small funnel to fill the burette with hydrochloric acid until past the zero point. This will make sure that when finding zero, the tip of the burette is full of liquid and has no air bubbles. Remove the funnel and level to zero, observing the meniscus at 90°.

Pipette 25.0 cm^3 of the solution of sodium carbonate into a conical flask and add two to three drops of methyl orange indicator. Record the initial volume of hydrochloric acid in the burette to two decimal places. Carry out a rough titration. Record the final volume of hydrochloric acid in the burette.

Repeat the titration until you obtain two titres within 0.20 cm^3. Note, it is unlikely you will have the time to carry out more than four titrations in total.

Results
The indicator colour changed from *yellow* to *pink*

Titration results for sodium carbonate against hydrochloric acid				
	Rough	1	2	3
Final burette reading/cm^3	33.50	23.70	24.00	23.20
Initial burette reading/cm^3	6.00	0.30	1.28	0.66
Volume of hydrochloric acid used/cm^3	27.50	23.40	22.72	22.54

Average titre / cm^3: *22.63*
The average titre was calculated using titres: *2 and 3*

It is good practice to repeat each experiment a few times to ensure that your results are reliable.

Always double-check any calculations to ensure they are correct before entering them neatly into a table as the learner has done here.

The learner has written out all the calculations, including the formulae, before coming up with the correct answer.

Worksheet 7: continued...

Calculations

1 Calculate the moles of sodium carbonate used in the titration.
(You know the concentration of the standard solution of sodium carbonate from the practical you undertook in Worksheet 6, and you have used 25.0 cm³ in this titration.)

$Moles = conc. \times vol \ (dm^3)$
$Vol = 25.00 /1000 = 0.025 \ dm^3$
$Moles = 0.056 \times 0.025 = 1.4 \times 10^{-3}$

2 Calculate the moles of hydrochloric acid used in the titration.
(You know the volume of HCl required for neutralisation and the concentration of the solution of HCl.)

$Moles = conc. \times vol \ (dm^3)$
$Vol = 22.63 /1000 = 0.02263 \ dm^3$
$Moles = 0.02263 \times 0.12 = 2.7156 \times 10^{-3}$

3 Calculate the ratio of the number of moles of HCl and Na_2CO_3 reacting.
2 mole(s) of HCl react(s) with 1 mole(s) of Na_2CO_3
$2.7156 \times 10^{-3} / 1.4 \times 10^{-3} = 1.94$

4 Write a balanced equation for the reaction between HCl and Na_2CO_3 remembering that a carbonate reacts with an acid to form a salt, carbon dioxide and water.

$Na_2CO_3 + 2 HCl \longrightarrow 2NaCl + CO_2 + H_2O$

Analysis

1 Do you think your results are reproducible? Give your reasoning.
The results should be reproducible using the same solutions.

2 Do you think that your results are accurate? Give your reasoning.
The results were fairly accurate having done them several times.
This reduces the risk of very inaccurate results.

3 What do you think are the major sources of error in this experiment?
Not reading the burette accurately.
Not seeing the colour change at exactly the right time.

Any symbol equations should be recorded as neatly and precisely as possible.

Concise and accurate answers are suitable in this context and fulfil the requirements for this part of P2.

Observation record (by tutor)

Learner name	Jason Evans
Qualification	BTEC Level 3 National Diploma in Applied Science
Unit number and title	Unit 1: Fundamentals of Science

Description of activity undertaken (please be as specific as possible)

The scenario required Jason to complete a number of worksheets for inclusion in a web-based educational presentation of teaching and learning resources on the use of titrations. P2 involved two practical investigations, preparing a standard solution of sodium carbonate and conducting a titration to determine the equation for the reaction between hydrochloric acid and sodium carbonate.

Assessment and grading criteria

P2: Demonstrate practically the ability to prepare chemical solutions and test their accuracy.

How the activity meets the requirements of the assessment and grading criteria

Jason read the instructions for the experiment before commencing his work and followed them carefully throughout his investigation. Although he initially brought unnecessary equipment to the work area, those items were subsequently returned. Health and safety guidance was studied and applied before commencing the investigation. After an initial breakage, the work was completed carefully. Accurate results were obtained. Upon completing the task the work area was cleaned and made safe.

Learner signature	Jason Evans	**Date**	1 December 2010
Assessor signature	John Morris	**Date**	1 December 2010
Assessor name	Mr J Morris		

Make sure that you sign and date any observation record forms to ensure that they are valid documents.

Sample learner work

This written information is necessary to provide some of the evidence for criterion M1.

The draft is well presented and laid out with just the correct amount of detail and it fulfils the evidence required for criterion M1.

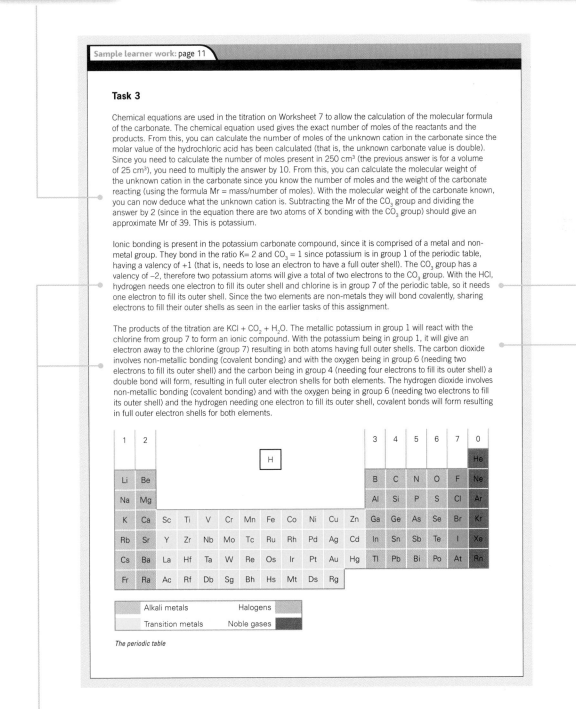

Sample learner work: page 11

Task 3

Chemical equations are used in the titration on Worksheet 7 to allow the calculation of the molecular formula of the carbonate. The chemical equation used gives the exact number of moles of the reactants and the products. From this, you can calculate the number of moles of the unknown cation in the carbonate since the molar value of the hydrochloric acid has been calculated (that is, the unknown carbonate value is double). Since you need to calculate the number of moles present in 250 cm³ (the previous answer is for a volume of 25 cm³), you need to multiply the answer by 10. From this, you can calculate the molecular weight of the unknown cation in the carbonate since you know the number of moles and the weight of the carbonate reacting (using the formula Mr = mass/number of moles). With the molecular weight of the carbonate known, you can now deduce what the unknown cation is. Subtracting the Mr of the CO_3 group and dividing the answer by 2 (since in the equation there are two atoms of X bonding with the CO_3 group) should give an approximate Mr of 39. This is potassium.

Ionic bonding is present in the potassium carbonate compound, since it is comprised of a metal and non-metal group. They bond in the ratio K= 2 and CO_3 = 1 since potassium is in group 1 of the periodic table, having a valency of +1 (that is, needs to lose an electron to have a full outer shell). The CO_3 group has a valency of –2, therefore two potassium atoms will give a total of two electrons to the CO_3 group. With the HCl, hydrogen needs one electron to fill its outer shell and chlorine is in group 7 of the periodic table, so it needs one electron to fill its outer shell. Since the two elements are non-metals they will bond covalently, sharing electrons to fill their outer shells as seen in the earlier tasks of this assignment.

The products of the titration are $KCl + CO_2 + H_2O$. The metallic potassium in group 1 will react with the chlorine from group 7 to form an ionic compound. With the potassium being in group 1, it will give an electron away to the chlorine (group 7) resulting in both atoms having full outer shells. The carbon dioxide involves non-metallic bonding (covalent bonding) and with the oxygen being in group 6 (needing two electrons to fill its outer shell) and the carbon being in group 4 (needing four electrons to fill its outer shell) a double bond will form, resulting in full outer electron shells for both elements. The hydrogen dioxide involves non-metallic bonding (covalent bonding) and with the oxygen being in group 6 (needing two electrons to fill its outer shell) and the hydrogen needing one electron to fill its outer shell, covalent bonds will form resulting in full outer electron shells for both elements.

The periodic table

The learner has made reference to the periodic table here, with evidence of links to previous work for P1 and P2.

The layout of this piece of work for D1 is very good. It has a title, includes several paragraphs and is clearly presented, the learner having checked for errors.

The content in this document is relevant to the evidence required for D1.

Sample learner work: page 12

Task 4

How are standard solutions prepared?

A standard solution is a solution whose concentration is known accurately. Its concentration is usually given in mol dm^{-3}. To find the concentrations of other substances in solution, a standard solution is used.

When making up the standard solution it is important that the correct mass of substance is accurately measured. It is also important that all of this is successfully transferred to the volumetric flask used to make up the solution accurately.

The acid titre can itself be used as a standard solution once its concentration has been determined by titrating against a known concentration of alkali solution.

Analysis of a chemical species can be achieved using **standard solutions**. Varying concentrations differ in their absorbance of light at particular wavelengths, and so a sample solution compared to various known standard solutions and their absorbances at certain wavelengths (using Beer's law) can be used to determine its concentration.

Standard solutions used in industry may have been prepared by another company and delivered to the testing point, or it may be part of the technician's job to prepare these solutions. These solutions themselves will undergo rigorous testing by the manufacturer or the technician to prove their accuracy before they can be used in the quality assurance of the products.

Using standard solutions, titrations of many types can be carried out.

The volumetric analysis
To determine the chemical differences of solutions in reactions, volumetric analysis is carried out. This type of analysis can also be used in oxidation/reduction (redox) reactions.

Titration
This is a technique used to find the volumes of solutions which react together. It is therefore called volumetric titration.

There are three types of volumetric titration:
• DTM – Direct Titration Method (single step process)
• ITM – Indirect Titration Method (two step process)
• BTM – Back Titration Method (three step process)

Principle
During a titration, a base and an acid will achieve equilibrium and the equation will be balanced. This is the principle of the method. Equilibrium occurs once the end-point is reached.

The process
A solution of analyte is prepared and added to a conical flask with a suitable indicator. The sample to be determined (titrant) is added drop by drop to the analyte until there is a change in colour.

The insertion of well-drawn and fully labelled illustrations can help to describe changes in scientific investigations.

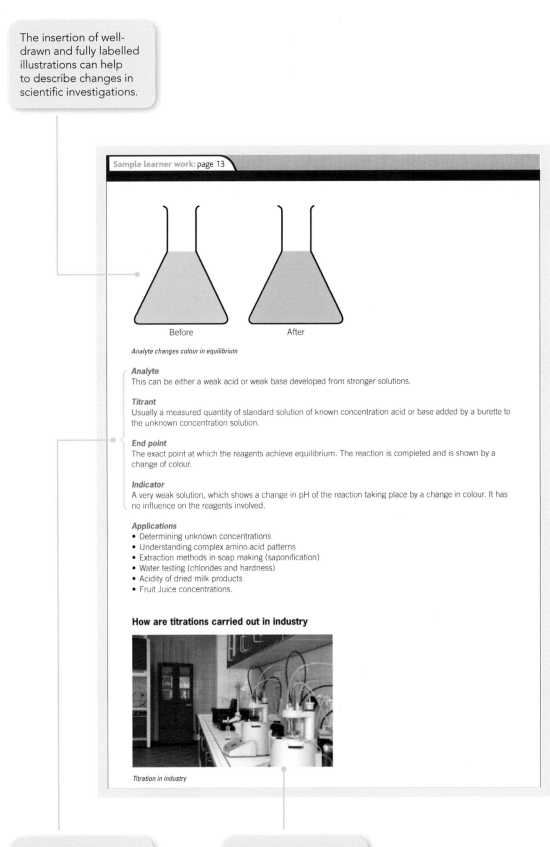

Sample learner work: page 13

Before   After

Analyte changes colour in equilibrium

Analyte
This can be either a weak acid or weak base developed from stronger solutions.

Titrant
Usually a measured quantity of standard solution of known concentration acid or base added by a burette to the unknown concentration solution.

End point
The exact point at which the reagents achieve equilibrium. The reaction is completed and is shown by a change of colour.

Indicator
A very weak solution, which shows a change in pH of the reaction taking place by a change in colour. It has no influence on the reagents involved.

Applications
- Determining unknown concentrations
- Understanding complex amino acid patterns
- Extraction methods in soap making (saponification)
- Water testing (chlorides and hardness)
- Acidity of dried milk products
- Fruit Juice concentrations.

How are titrations carried out in industry

Titration in industry

The learner has added these relevant scientific definitions to help to fulfil the evidence requirements for D1.

The use of photographs that are related to this part of the investigation has helped to inform the draft.

Research using various relevant websites, books and journals enables the learner to respond to the task in an informed manner.

Sample learner work: page 14

There are many different reasons why a titration might be carried out in industry. In the waste oil industry oil titration is an indicator test for free fatty acids (FFA) in restaurant fryer oil, which only takes 30 seconds to titrate. It is done by reacting a small sample of the FFA with a measured amount of lye using pH to indicate when the FFA is all used up.

FFA is an acid produced by the heating and cooking of food with oil over time. As FFA accumulates it causes used vegetable oil to become more and more acidic. Oil which has been overheated or over-used can turn into a product that has been implicated in cancer.

Variations on these titrations are used in the petrochemical industry to define the differences in acidity of waste oil that is to become biodiesel. This process is becoming increasingly popular as the price of oil and petrol is rising rapidly.

Titrations are carried out in many industries including the water industry, in which they are used to check the quality of our drinking water; the dairy industry, for testing milk and cheese products; and the pharmaceutical industry, for checking the quality of drugs on the production line, to name just a few of their industrial applications. Titration in industry for different types of investigation need to be extremely precise and consistent compared to the class titration. The major difference between titrations in industry is that they may use machinery that is capable of delivering the exact amount of reactant needed and other equipment to perform the process. These processes may take place without the need for intervention of laboratory staff. It also means that the machine is able to read the results for the end point down to minute fractions and therefore, be incredibly precise.

Chemical analysis in industry

In industry the theory behind the simple volumetric titration is exactly the same as has been investigated in this practical work. Although the industrial production scale may be very large the laboratory testing and quality assurance may be on a small scale and may still be done manually although it will be going on at all times and covering different points in the manufacturing process. Some examples of the processes associated with titration in industry will include the simple manual addition of titrant to analyte with the addition of an indicator where the end point is determined by eye. Sugar and salt determinations are commonly performed in food laboratories using manual colourmetric end point titrations but can suffer from the production of colour during the reactions so masking the indicator making the end point difficult to see. However some processes must be monitored continuously to monitor the progress of the process.

Where titrations are required on a continuous basis, instrument manufacturers can provide a complete system, which includes an ion selective electrode, reference electrode, electrode head, pH electrode, temperature sensor, electrode-computer interface, and ion analyser software.

An illustration of scientific equipment used for titrations helps to inform the explanation.

The applications of titration are explained to provide evidence for D1.

Applications include:
- water quality analysis of surface and ground waters, fish ponds, aquaculture, sewage, and industrial effluent
- food and drink quality control, bio-reactors and fermentors
- monitoring of the progress of the process of alcohol production for both industrial use and consumption;
- pharmaceutical, agricultural and medical research.

In the pharmaceutical and cosmetic industries, surfactants (anionic, cationic and non-ionic) are used to allow substances to flow or spread more easily by reducing the surface tension of water within it. The quality and content of the surfactant can be determined by suitable applied methods of titration.

For each type of industry manufacturers will produce automated equipment to meet the specific needs of the processes being carried out. All of these processes may not be using titration but will be monitoring production and processing.

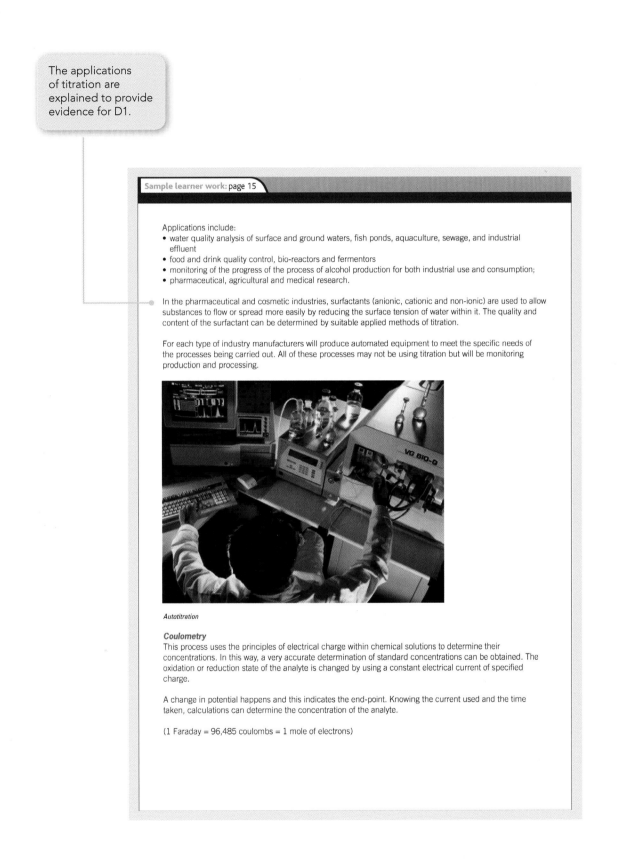

Autotitration

Coulometry

This process uses the principles of electrical charge within chemical solutions to determine their concentrations. In this way, a very accurate determination of standard concentrations can be obtained. The oxidation or reduction state of the analyte is changed by using a constant electrical current of specified charge.

A change in potential happens and this indicates the end-point. Knowing the current used and the time taken, calculations can determine the concentration of the analyte.

(1 Faraday = 96,485 coulombs = 1 mole of electrons)

Illustrations can be created using a computer to show how different titration processes work.

The information given is detailed and explains every aspect of each process.

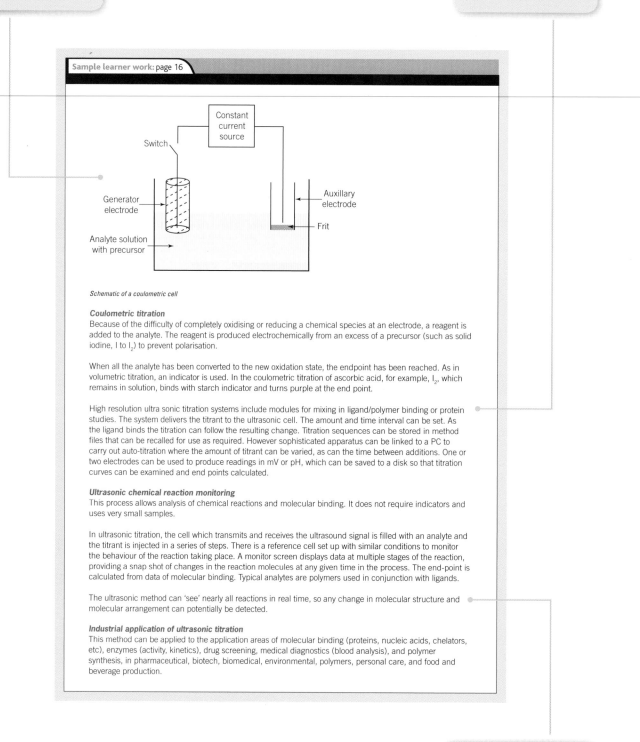

Sample learner work: page 16

Schematic of a coulometric cell

Coulometric titration

Because of the difficulty of completely oxidising or reducing a chemical species at an electrode, a reagent is added to the analyte. The reagent is produced electrochemically from an excess of a precursor (such as solid iodine, I to I_2) to prevent polarisation.

When all the analyte has been converted to the new oxidation state, the endpoint has been reached. As in volumetric titration, an indicator is used. In the coulometric titration of ascorbic acid, for example, I_2, which remains in solution, binds with starch indicator and turns purple at the end point.

High resolution ultra sonic titration systems include modules for mixing in ligand/polymer binding or protein studies. The system delivers the titrant to the ultrasonic cell. The amount and time interval can be set. As the ligand binds the titration can follow the resulting change. Titration sequences can be stored in method files that can be recalled for use as required. However sophisticated apparatus can be linked to a PC to carry out auto-titration where the amount of titrant can be varied, as can the time between additions. One or two electrodes can be used to produce readings in mV or pH, which can be saved to a disk so that titration curves can be examined and end points calculated.

Ultrasonic chemical reaction monitoring

This process allows analysis of chemical reactions and molecular binding. It does not require indicators and uses very small samples.

In ultrasonic titration, the cell which transmits and receives the ultrasound signal is filled with an analyte and the titrant is injected in a series of steps. There is a reference cell set up with similar conditions to monitor the behaviour of the reaction taking place. A monitor screen displays data at multiple stages of the reaction, providing a snap shot of changes in the reaction molecules at any given time in the process. The end-point is calculated from data of molecular binding. Typical analytes are polymers used in conjunction with ligands.

The ultrasonic method can 'see' nearly all reactions in real time, so any change in molecular structure and molecular arrangement can potentially be detected.

Industrial application of ultrasonic titration

This method can be applied to the application areas of molecular binding (proteins, nucleic acids, chelators, etc), enzymes (activity, kinetics), drug screening, medical diagnostics (blood analysis), and polymer synthesis, in pharmaceutical, biotech, biomedical, environmental, polymers, personal care, and food and beverage production.

Each titration process is presented in similar detail and order. This is good practice when completing such assignments.

Ultrasonic titration

Automation ensures uniformity in technique producing analytical data of consistently high quality. It eliminates the need for labour intensive manual measurements saving time and costs with increased productivity.

In the process of potentiometric titration direct measurement is of benefit with a high sample throughput or with a known sample solution of a simple composition. Standard addition is recommended where a determination is only carried out occasionally or when the composition of the sample is unknown. Two electrodes are always used, one being the measuring or indicator electrode and the other called the reference electrode.

Amperometric titration

Where coulometric titration applies an electrical current for a given time, amperometric titration involves the measurement of the electrical current produced at end-point of the reaction. It is, therefore, a form of quantitative analysis.

Example – an electrolytic potential is applied to an analyte solution and conductive buffer. The measured electrical current can be used to determine the concentration of the analyte since the concentration affects conductivity. This is a form of amperometry.

However, the amount of electrical current is also dependent on other factors which are not all easily controllable. This may account for a lack of precision in this method of analysis.

The analyte concentration is subject to variations which are directly linked to the applied electrical potential. This is more noticeable at close proximity to the electrode where analyte reduction can take place more readily than at areas away from the electrode.

The concentration of the analyte will, therefore, depend on the rate of diffusion of the analyte. Another factor which will affect the analyte concentration is the relative size of the electrode compared to the volume of analyte.

Industrial applications of different titration processes are evident.

A decrease in the current produced by reduction of lead ions in an analyte can be seen to occur if another chemical species is added which reacts to the lead ion, eg chromate ions. As more chromate is added, the current drops in accordance with continued reduction of lead ions at the electrode. A graph plotted of current against volume of added titrant should produce a straight line.

The gradient of the straight line will change when the reaction of chromate ions (titrant) and lead ions is complete. Excess titrant will now reduce at the electrode. The change in slope marks the end-point of the reaction.

By altering the electrode potential, it is possible to allow reduction of titrant and not analyte. Excess titrant will show as an increase in current above the background current.

Industrial application of amperometric titration

This type of titration is used to analyse the contaminants such as zinc and zinc salts in the manufacture of theophylline for pharmaceutical use. Such contaminants prevent the use of other equipment in the manufacturing process.

Photometric titration

This is a titration in which the titrant and solution cause the formation of a metal complex accompanied by an observable change in light absorbance by the titrated solution.

When light is used as the principal form of analysis, it is essential to select an appropriate wavelength for analysis, since all components in a titration (titrant, analyte and products) absorb light. Every effort is made to select a wavelength absorbed by only one component. The part of the molecule responsible for producing this light (chromophore) must follow Beer's law at this particular wavelength. This means that there is a change in the observed absorbance characteristic as the concentration of the absorbing species changes. A graph of absorbance against titrant volume should produce a straight line.

The chromophore concentration changes up to the point of equivalence but does not change any further even when more titrant is added.

Two straight lines produced on the graph, absorbance/titrant volume up to the end point and absorbance/titrant volume beyond the end point, will intersect at the equivalence point.

The accuracy of this method is brought into question when absorbance levels are very high. Consequently, percentage transmittance (%T) of the selected wavelength is low, and so it is desirable to choose lower analyte concentrations, a buffer and wavelengths associated with slow absorbance changes.

Industrial application of photometric titration

Both tartaric acid and citric acid are products of the fermentation process. Acid-base titration, using phenolphthalein indicator, is widely used for the total acidity determination in wine.

Automated titration has greatly evolved by employing the flow injection analysis process to handle solutions and detection by spectrophotometry

As well as the laboratory personnel carrying out small scale testing, each industry will have its own specialised instrumentation to monitor and adjust the processes automatically.

Conductivity titration

Unlike the photometric titration, conductivity titrations do not use indicators but electrical charge.

This form of titration produces a curved plot of conductance against volume of sodium hydroxide (NaOH). When titrating a strong base with a strong acid, conductance falls considerably at the end-point, which is then used as an indicator measure.

The learner has made reference to the accuracy of this process.

Industrial application of conductivity titration

For use in situations where a strong acid and strong base are in use and where an indicator colour may be masked by the titrant, analyte or its products.

Visual or photometric indication titration relies on the colour change in the range of the indicator. Temperature can considerably affect the end point of a titration so solutions must be kept at a constant temperature if consistent results are to be obtained. This will require monitoring and control if automatic testing is being undertaken.

Sample assessor's comments

It is valuable to self-reflect on your assignment work. This includes looking at aspects that you enjoyed and that went well, as well as areas that you found difficult.

The assessor will note a Y (Yes) or an N (No) next to each of the grading criteria to indicate whether you have achieved it or not.

Qualification	BTEC Level 3 National Diploma in Applied Science	Year	2010–2011
Unit number and title	Unit 1: Fundamentals of Science	Learner name	Jason Evans

Grading criteria	Achieved?
P1 outline the key features of the periodic table, atomic structure and chemical bonding	Y
P2 demonstrate practically the ability to prepare chemical solutions and test their accuracy	Y
M1 relate the key features of the periodic table to the conclusions drawn from the practical activities	Y
D1 explain how standard solutions and titrations are prepared in industry	Y

Learner feedback

I worked hard on this assignment but I did find it difficult to obtain information on the industrial uses of titrations.

Assessor feedback

You have successfully provided evidence using the worksheets provided for P1 in Task 1 and 2, identifying and describing the atomic structure, information from the periodic table, bonding and titration. You have carried out the practical work in a safe and accurate manner for P2. In Task 3 you produced some valid conclusions from the practical work. Finally you have written succinctly about the preparation of standard solutions and how titrations are carried out in industry. D1 has therefore been achieved. An excellent assignment.

Action plan

Continue to read generally around the subject and build on your very good work.

Assessor signature	J Morris	Date	19 January 2011
Learner signature	Jason Evans	Date	19 January 2011

The action plan gives advice on ways to improve future work.

Step Seven: Work productively as a member of a group

Case study: : Crime Scene Investigation Teams

As part of the BTEC Level 3 National Diploma in Applied Science (Forensic Science) course, a class of learners is asked to work together in teams of four to complete a task. Their assignment is entitled 'Crime Scene Investigation'. Each group has to work as a forensic-science research team to analyse and discuss a 'Who killed Kennedy' scenario. They are required to produce a report which could be given to the police to use as evidence in court. This should contain vital evidence about the murder scene and suspect. The class is asked to complete the group task for homework.

Two groups have very different experiences of the task which are reported below.

Group 1 – Louise selects herself as team leader. She tells her group members what they each need to do. Leah and Dennis aren't happy with Louise's approach and Ayden hates the fact that she won't let him make any decisions. Ayden becomes fed up and won't do the job Louise has given him, which is to measure the blood splats found at the crime scene. Leah and Dennis are told to analyse fingerprints found at the crime scene, while Louise says she will supervise the others in their tasks. Ayden becomes disruptive and stops the others working. Louise shouts at him and is upset that he won't participate.

Group 2 – Stephan suggests the group vote for a team leader. The group agrees he should be leader as he is fair. The team members set about tasks given to them by Stephan, having listened to each other's views on what jobs need to be done and what the report should include. They make a very good start on their tasks and arrange to meet up in the library after lessons at 4pm on Thursdays to complete the assignment. Finally, they swap email addresses and phone numbers, and Stephan asks his group to agree an agenda for the next meeting.

Reflection points

Think about your involvement in team situations. Do you usually speak out more that you observe and listen? Or vice versa?

Think about why a team needs a leader. How would you choose a team leader?

In your private life, you can choose your own friends, whereas at work you are paid to work alongside many people; whether you like them or not.

This applies at school or college too. Hopefully, by now, you've outgrown wanting to only work with your best friends on every project.

You may not be keen on everyone in your team, but you should still be pleasant and cooperative. This may be harder if you are working with a partner than in a large group.

Sometimes you may be the group leader. This may inspire you, or fill you with dread. You won't be expected to develop team-leader skills overnight, but it helps if you know the basics.

First, you should understand how groups and teams work and why good teamwork is considered vital by employers.

Working in groups and teams

If you have a full- or part-time job, you already belong to a working group, or team. At school or college your class is an example of a working group.

All working groups have some common characteristics:

- doing the same type of work – though in the workplace you probably have different roles or responsibilities
- a group leader or supervisor
- a reason for working together, such as studying for the same qualification or tackling an area of work too large for someone to do alone
- group members are dependent on each other in some way; at work you may have to cover someone's workload if they are absent
- group members concentrate on their individual achievements and success.

A team is different. As a team member you have a specific objective to achieve **together** – and this is more important than the goals of individual team members.

TOP TIP

Understanding how groups and teams function will help you be a better team worker and a better team leader.

These are the characteristics of a team.

- Team members have a team goal which is more important than any personal goals.
- Team members have complementary skills so that the team can achieve more than individuals working alone could achieve.
- Work is allocated to play to each person's strengths and talents.
- The team members give each other encouragement and support.
- There is collective responsibility for achieving the goal.

A good team leader acts as facilitator and motivator, and gives practical support and guidance.

Working in a team has many benefits. Team members can learn from each other and combine their skills to do a better job more quickly. Working with other people is often more enjoyable than working alone, too. Many industries rely heavily on efficient group working, from IT teams to health workers and the emergency services.

TOP TIP

Focusing on the task rather than on personalities is the first step in learning to work with different people, whose views may not match your own.

There are many benefits to be gained from working as a team.

Being a good team member

Everyone wants team members who are talented, positive, cheerful and full of energy. These are the key areas to focus on if you wish to be a good team member.

- **Your social skills.** This includes being courteous, treating other people as you wish to be treated, saying 'please' when you want something and thanking people who do you a favour.

- **Your temperament**. Expect people to have different views and opinions from you and don't take offence if someone disagrees with you. If you lose your temper easily, learn to walk away before you say something you may regret.

- **Your communication skills.** This includes talking and listening!

- Practise saying what you mean clearly, accurately and succinctly. Be prepared to give good reasons to justify your arguments and ideas.
  Allow people to finish what they're saying, without interruption, before you talk. Never shout people down. Think before you speak so that you don't upset people with tactless remarks. If you inadvertently do so, apologise.

- **Your commitment.** Always keep your promises and never let anyone down when they are depending upon you. Always do your fair share of the work, even if you don't agree with all the decisions made by your team. Tell people promptly if you are having problems so there is time to solve them. Be loyal to your team when you're talking to other people.

Being the team leader

It can be difficult to strike a balance between 'leading' the team and working with friends. You need to inspire and motivate your team without being bossy or critical.

Important points to remember about being a team leader

- Lead by example. Stay pleasant, consistent and control your temper, even under pressure.
- Everyone is different. Your ways of working may not always be the best.
- Be prepared to listen and contribute positively to a discussion.
- Encourage quieter team members to join in discussions by asking for their views.
- Be prepared to do whatever you ask other people to do.
- Note down what you say you will do, so that you don't forget.
- Discuss alternatives with people rather than giving orders.
- Be sensitive to other people's feelings. They may have personal problems or issues that affect their behaviour.
- Learn the art of persuasion.
- Act as peacemaker. Help people reach a compromise when necessary.
- Give team members the credit for their hard work or good ideas.
- Admit your mistakes. Look for a positive solution and think about what can be learned for the future, rather than making excuses.
- Praise and encourage team members who are working hard.
- Make criticisms constructively, and in private.
- Be assertive (put forward your point of view firmly) rather than aggressive (attacking other people to defend yourself).

Some notes of caution about being a team leader

- Try to look pleasant and don't glare at people who interrupt you unexpectedly.
- Never talk about team members behind their backs.
- Don't gossip, exaggerate to make a point, spread rumours, speculate or tell lies.
- Don't expect to get your own way all the time – all good leaders back down on occasion.
- Never criticise any colleagues in front of other people. Speak to them in private and keep it constructive.

TOP TIP

Excellent ideas often come from quiet team members. Encourage everyone to make suggestions so that you don't overlook any valuable contributions.

Key points

- There are many benefits of working in a group or as a team. These include mutual support, companionship and the exchange of ideas.
- You will be expected to work cooperatively with other people at work, and during many course assignments.
- It isn't easy learning to be a team leader. Team leaders should be fair, consistent and pleasant to work with, as well as loyal and sensitive to the needs of team members.

Action points

1 Identify the role of teamwork in your area of study. Identify the team's goal and any factors you think will contribute towards its success.

2 Decide how you would handle each of the following difficult situations if you were the team leader. If you can, discuss your ideas with a friend in your class.

a) The team needs to borrow a college video camera to record an event being held tonight. Your tutor tells you that the one you reserved last week is not working and the rest are out on loan.

b) A member of your team has personal problems so you have given him less work to do. Now you've been accused of having favourites.

c) A team member is constantly letting everyone down because of poor work and non-attendance at group meetings.

d) Two team members have disagreed about how to do a task. You're not bothered how they do it as long as it gets done properly, and by the deadline.

e) A team member becomes very aggressive whenever she is challenged in any way – no matter how mildly.

3 Identify someone who has inspired you because they've been an excellent leader. This could be someone you've met, a fictional character or a famous person. Note down what it is about them that impressed you.

TOP TIP

Team working, and bouncing ideas around, produces quicker and better results than working in isolation.

Activity: A good team leader

Most careers in science require you to be involved in team meetings. Meetings might be held to discuss what has been done, what needs to improve or to find better ways of working in the future. As you progress in your chosen science-related career, you might become a team leader. This will involve more responsibility; you will have to ensure that your team members are working well together, being productive, making improvements and following health and safety guidelines.

Look at this scenario. Thinking about how a good team leader should act, select the correct answer for each question. Use pages 68–69 of this guide to help you.

Scenario

You are a team leader in a cancer research department and you have called a meeting to discuss how your team has done so far in developing a new treatment for breast cancer.

1 You come into the laboratory for the meeting and sit down to speak to your team. Would you:

   a) be pleasant and ask each member of the team to tell the rest of the group about the results of their individual research into the new treatment?

   b) tell them that you know the best way to get the treatment to work, and that you don't want to hear if they haven't yet proved it?

2 One member of the team interrupts you as you are talking. He feels strongly that another team member is not doing her work correctly. Would you:

   a) glare and shout at him not to interrupt you while you are speaking?

   b) behave assertively and sensitively, saying that you will discuss this issue in private after the meeting?

3 You realise that you made a mistake when telling your team about some of the health and safety issues related to the new treatment. Would you:

   a) fail to admit your mistake and hope that the team members find this information out for themselves?

   b) tell the team that you have made a mistake and inform them about the consequences on human health when using this treatment?

4 Your team has worked extremely hard and is well on the way to developing a new treatment for breast cancer. Would you:

   a) criticise them for making slow progress saying, 'We should have completed the work by now.'?

   b) praise your team for all their hard work while reminding them, with offers of assistance, that they have a deadline to meet?

Step Eight: Understand how to research and analyse information

Case study: Finding and analysing information for an assignment

Liam has been given his first assignment on the BTEC Level 3 National Subsidiary Diploma in Applied Science course. He is determined to get a distinction for his work. Liam wants to work in bioinformatics in the future and so needs high grades to get into university.

Liam's tutor delivers the introductory lesson. This covers the pass criteria for the assignment entitled 'Cardiovascular and Respiratory Function'. Liam makes lots of notes on A4 paper, jotting down the bits he thinks are important and highlighting words which are new to him. He then files his notes carefully.

In the second lesson, Liam has to complete an investigation into the effects of exercise on the cardiovascular and respiratory systems. For the merit and distinction criteria, he has to use his primary research and compare it to secondary data from another scientific investigation.

Following the lesson, Liam goes to the library with his assignment brief and starts to collect some resources. He gathers books from a reading list given to him by his tutor and does an advanced search on the internet. He is looking for the secondary data to address the merit and distinction criteria. He saves the useful websites into his 'My Favourites' box for later reference. Liam also reads through some journals and newspaper articles, and makes some notes of references which he could add to his work later.

Having collected all this information, Liam then scan reads each source. He questions whether each one is relevant to the learning outcomes for his assignment. He soon narrows down his resources. Liam reads in detail each selected source to make sure he understands it and checks any new words using a dictionary. He then makes a note of the key points to jog his memory.

Liam finally completes his assignment in good time for the deadline. He proofreads his work to make sure he has included everything and hasn't made any errors. He then asks his friend to read his essay to make sure that there are no final mistakes, before submitting his assignment for the deadline date.

Reflection points

Think about how you research information. Are your current techniques effective?

As a BTEC Level 3 National learner, you often have to find information for yourself. This skill will be invaluable in your working life, and if you continue your studies at higher education (HE) level. Sometimes the information will give you a better understanding of a topic, at other times you will research to obtain information for a project or assignment. Sometimes you may be so interested in something that you want to find out more without being told to do so!

Whatever your reason, and no matter where your information can be found, there is a good and not so good way to go about the task. This section will help if you can't find what you want, or find too much, or drift aimlessly around a library, or watch a demonstration and don't know what to ask afterwards.

Types of information

There are many types of information and many different sources. Depending on the task, these are the sources you may need to consult.

- **Verbal information.** This includes talking to friends, colleagues at work, members of your family, listening to experts explain what they do, interviewing people, talking to sales reps at an exhibition or customers about a product.

- **Printed information.** This includes information printed in newspapers, journals, magazines, books, posters, workshop manuals, leaflets and catalogues. The type of magazine or newspaper you read may have its own slant on the information, which you may have to take into account (see page 81).

- **Written information.** This includes course notes and handouts, reports and other documents in the workplace. If you want to use written information from work, you must check this is allowed, and that it doesn't contain confidential material such as financial information or staff names and addresses.

- **Graphical information.** This includes illustrations, pictures, cartoons, line drawings, graphs and photographs. Graphics can make something clearer than words alone. For example, a satnav instruction book might contain illustrations to show different procedures.

- **Electronic information.** This includes information from electronic sources such as DVDs, CD-ROMs, searchable databases, websites, podcasts, webinars (**seminars** online), emails and text messages. The huge amount of information available online is both a help and a hindrance. You can find information quickly, but the source may be unreliable, out-of-date, inaccurate or inappropriate (see pages 74–75.)

TOP TIP

Too much information is as bad as too little, because it's overwhelming. The trick is to find good quality, relevant information and know when to call a halt to your search.

TOP TIP

Consider all appropriate sources and don't just rely on information found online.

Finding what you need

Spend a few minutes planning what to do before you start looking for information. This can save a lot of time later on.

The following steps will help you to do this.

1 Make sure you understand exactly what it is you need to know so that you don't waste time looking for the wrong thing.

2 Clarify your objectives to narrow down your search. Think about why the information is wanted and how much detail you need. For example, learners studying BTEC Nationals in Engineering and Performing Arts may both be researching 'noise' for their projects but they are likely to need different types of information and use it in different ways.

3 Identify your sources and check you know how to use them. You need to choose sources that are most likely to provide information relevant to your objectives. For example, an Engineering learner might find information on noise emissions in industry journals and by checking out specialist websites.

4 Plan and schedule your research. Theoretically, you could research information forever. Knowing when to call a halt takes skill. Write a schedule that states when you must stop looking and start sorting the information.

5 Store your information safely in a labelled folder. This folder should include printouts or photocopies of articles, notes about events you have attended or observed, photographs you've taken or sketches you've drawn. Divide your information under topic headings to make it easier to find. When you're ready to start work, re-read your assignment brief and select the items that are most closely related to the task you are doing.

Primary and secondary research, and the law of copyright

There are two ways to research information. One is known as primary research, the other is secondary research.

Primary research

Primary research involves finding new information about an issue or topic. This might include finding out people's views about a product or interviewing an expert. When carrying out interviews, you will need to design a survey or questionnaire. Your primary research might also include observing or experiencing something for yourself, and recording your feelings and observations.

Secondary research

Secondary research involves accessing information that already exists in books, files, newspapers or on CD-ROMs, computer databases or the internet, and assessing it against your objectives.

This information has been prepared by other people and is available to anyone. You can quote from an original work provided you acknowledge the source of your information. You should put this acknowledgement in your text or in the bibliography to your text; do not claim it as your own research. You must include the author's name, year of publication, the title and publisher, or the web address if it is an online article. You should practise listing the sources of articles so

that you feel confident writing a bibliography. Use the guidance sheet issued by your centre to help you. This will illustrate the style your centre recommends. (See also page 10.)

The trick with research is to choose the best technique to achieve your objectives and this may mean using a mix of methods and resources. For example, if you have to comment on an industry event you might go to it, make notes, interview people attending, observe the event (perhaps take a video camera), and read any newspaper reports or online comments.

People as a source of information

If you want to get the most out of interviewing someone, or several people, you need to prepare carefully in advance.

The following points give some general advice about getting the most out of face-to-face interviews.

- Make sure you know what questions to ask to get the information you need.
- Explain why you want the information.
- Don't expect to be told confidential or sensitive information.
- Write clear notes so that you remember who told you what, and when. (See also page 76.)
- Note the contact details of the person you are interviewing and ask whether they mind if you contact them again should you think of anything later or need to clarify your notes.
- Thank them for their help.

If you want to ask a lot of people for their opinion you may want to conduct a survey. You will need to design a questionnaire and analyse the results. This will be easier if you ask for **quantitative** responses – for example yes/no, true/false or ratings on a five-point scale – rather than opinions.

- Give careful thought to your representative sample (people whose opinions are relevant to the topic).
- Decide how many people to survey so that the results mean something.
- Keep the survey relatively short.
- Thank people who complete it.
- Analyse the results, and write up your conclusions promptly.

TOP TIP

Test your questionnaire on volunteers before you 'go live' to check that there are no mistakes and the questions are easy to understand. Make any amendments before you conduct your 'real' survey.

Asking someone who knows a lot about a topic can be informative.

Avoiding pitfalls

Wikipedia is a good online source that covers many topics, and often in some depth. It is popular and free. However, it has an open-content policy, which means that anyone can contribute to and edit entries. People may post information, whether it is correct or not. Wikipedia is moving towards greater checks on entries, but it is still sensible to check out information you find on this site somewhere else.

Apart from inaccuracy, you may find other problems with information you obtain through research, especially material found online.

- **Out-of-date material.** Check the date of everything and keep only the latest version of books, newspapers or magazines. Yesterday's news may be of little use if you are researching something topical.
- **Irrelevant details.** Often, only part of an article will be relevant to your search. For example, if you are forecasting future trends in an area of work, you do not need information about its history or related problems. When learners are struggling, they sometimes 'pad out' answers with irrelevant information. If you've researched properly you can avoid this by having enough relevant information for your purposes.

- **Invalid assumptions.** This means someone has jumped to the wrong conclusion and made 2 + 2 = 5. You might do this if you see two friends chatting and think they are talking about you – whether they are or not! You can avoid problems in this area by double-checking your ideas and getting evidence to support them.

- **Bias.** This is when people hold strong views about a topic, or let their emotions or prejudices affect their judgement. An obvious example is asking a keen football fan for an objective evaluation of their team's performance!

- **Vested interests.** People may argue in a certain way because it's in their own interests to do so. For example, when the Government said Home Information Packs must be prepared for all properties being sold, the Association of Home Information Pack Providers was in favour because it trains the people who prepare the packs. The National Association of Estate Agents and Royal Institution of Chartered Surveyors were not because they thought they would lose business if people were put off selling their houses.

TOP TIP

Don't discard information that is affected by bias or vested interests. Just make it clear you know about the problem and have taken it into account.

Reading for a purpose

You may enjoy reading or you may find it tedious or difficult. If so, it helps to know that there are different ways to read, depending on what you're doing. For example, you wouldn't look for a programme in a TV guide in the same way that you would check an assignment for mistakes. You can save time and find information more easily if you use the best method of reading to suit your purpose. The following are some examples of ways of reading.

- **Skim reading** is used to check new information and get a general overview. To skim a book chapter read the first and last paragraphs, the headings, subheadings and illustrations. It also helps to read the first sentence of each paragraph.

TOP TIP

News articles are written with the key points at the beginning, so concentrate on the first paragraph or two. Feature articles have a general introduction and important information is contained in the main text.

- **Scanning** is used to see whether an article contains something you need – such as key words, dates or technical terms. Focus on capital or initial letters for a name, and figures for a date. Technical terms may be in bold or italics.

- **Light reading** is usually done for pleasure when you are relaxed, for example, reading a magazine article. You may not remember many facts afterwards, so this sort of reading isn't suitable for learning something or assessing its value.

- **Word-by-word reading (proofreading)** is important so that you don't miss anything, such as the dosage instructions for a strong medicine. You should proofread assignments before you submit them.

- **Reading for study (active reading)** means being actively involved so that you understand the information. It is rare to be naturally good at this, so you might have to work to develop this skill.

Developing critical and analytical skills

Developing critical and analytical skills involves looking at information for any flaws in the arguments. These skills are important when you progress to work or higher education (HE), so it's useful to practise them now on your BTEC Level 3 National course.

A useful technique for understanding, analysing, evaluating and remembering what you are reading is **SQ4R**.

SQ4R is an effective method. It consists of six steps.

1 **Survey** first, to get a general impression. Scan the information to see what it is about, when it was written and by whom. The source, and the reason it was written, may be important. Most newspapers, for example, have their own 'slant' that affects how information is presented.

2 **Question** your aims for reading this material. What are you hoping to find? What questions are you expecting it to answer?

3 **Read** the information three or four times. The first time, aim to get a general idea of the content. Use a dictionary to look up any new words. Then read more carefully to understand what the writer really means.

4 **Respond** by thinking critically about the information and how it relates to the topic you are studying. Does it answer your queries partially, fully or not at all? What information is factual and what is based on opinion? Is there evidence to support these opinions? Is there a reason why the author has taken this standpoint? Do you agree with it? How does it link to other information you have read? What is the opposite argument and is there any evidence to support this? Overall, how useful is this information?

5 **Record** the information by noting the key points. Use this to refresh your memory, if necessary, rather than re-reading the article.

6 **Review** your notes against the original to check you have included all important points. If you are also preparing a presentation, reviewing your notes will help you to remember key points more easily.

TOP TIP

SQ4R is just one method of reading for study. Research others and adapt them to suit your own style.

Taking good notes

There are many occasions when you need to take notes, such as when a visiting speaker is talking to your class. There's no point taking notes unless you write them in a way that will allow you to use them later.

Note-taking is a personal activity. Some people prefer to make diagrammatical sketches with key points in boxes linked by arrows; others prefer to write a series of bullet points. You will develop your own style, but the following hints and tips might help you at the start.

- Use A4 lined paper, rather than a notebook, so that you have more space and don't need to turn over so often.

- When you're reading for study, make sure you have a dictionary, pen, notepad and highlighter to hand.

- Leave a wide margin to record your own comments or queries.

- Put a heading at the top, such as the speaker's name and topic, as well as the date.

- If you are making notes from a book or an article, remember SQ4R and read it several times first. Your notes will only be effective if you understand the information.

- Don't write in complete sentences – it takes too long.

- Leave spaces for later additions or corrections.

- Use headings to keep your notes clear and well organised.

- Only write down relevant information, including key words and phrases.

- Highlight, underline or use capitals for essential points.
- Never copy chunks of text – always use your own words.
- Clearly identify quotations, and record your sources, so that you can cite them in your work. (Note the author's name, title, publisher, date and place of publication and the page number.)

TOP TIP

Make sure your information is accurate, up-to-date, relevant and valid. Be aware of bias, and don't confuse fact with opinion.

Key points

- Useful information may be verbal, printed, written, graphical or electronic.
- Effective research means knowing exactly what you are trying to find and where to look. Know how reference media are stored in your library and how to search online. Store important information carefully.
- Primary research is original data you obtain yourself. Secondary research is information prepared by someone else. If you use this, you must quote your sources in a bibliography.
- You can search for information by skimming and scanning, and read in different ways. Reading for study means actively involving yourself with the text, questioning what you are reading and making notes to help your own understanding.
- Read widely around a topic to get different viewpoints. Don't accept everything you read as correct. Think about how it fits with other information you have obtained.
- Taking notes is a personal skill that takes time to develop. Start by using A4 lined pages with a margin, set out your notes clearly and label them. Only record essential information.

Action points

- Working with a friend, look back at the sources of information listed on page 72. For each type, identify examples of information relevant to your course that you could obtain from each source. See how many you can list under each type.
- Check your ability to find the information you need by answering each of the questions in **Activity: Finding information** on the next page. For any questions you get wrong, your first research task is to find out the correct answers as quickly as you can.
- To check your ability to skim and scan information, improve your ability to differentiate fact from opinion, summarise text and much more, go to page 104 to see how to access useful websites.
- Check your ability to sort fact from opinion and spot vested interests by completing **Activity: Let's give you a tip…** on pages 80–81. Check your ideas with the answers on page 103.

TOP TIP

Make a note of any information that you are struggling to understand so that you can discuss it with your tutor.

Activity: Finding information

Answer the following questions about finding information.

a) Four types of information that are available from the library in your centre, besides books, are:

1

2

3

4

b) When I visit the library, the way to check if a book I want is available is:

c) The difference between borrowing a book on short-term loan and on long-term loan is:

Short-term loan:

Long-term loan:

d) The journals that are stocked by the library that are relevant to my course include:

e) Useful information on the intranet at my centre includes:

f) Searchable databases and online magazines I can access include:

g) The quickest way to check if a book or journal contains the type of information I need is to:

h) The difference between a search engine, a portal, a directory site and a forum is:

i) Bookmarking useful websites means:

j) In addition to suggesting websites, Google can also provide the following types of information:

k) Specialist websites which provide useful information related to my course include:

l) Useful tips I would give to people starting on my course who need to find out information are:

Activity: Let's give you a tip...

In 2009, many businesses were struggling thanks to the credit crunch and falling consumer demand. Some, like Woolworths, closed down altogether. Others laid off staff, or announced wage cuts. Despite this, the Government approved recommendations by the Low Pay Commission to increase the minimum wage rate from October 2009. Although the rise was only small, many unions, including Unison and Usdaw, agreed it was better than a freeze, which had been wanted by the British Chambers of Commerce and the British Retail Consortium.

The Government also announced new laws to stop restaurants and bars using tips to top up staff pay to the minimum level. *The Independent* newspaper claimed its 'fair tips, fair pay' campaign had won the day. It also reported that the British Hospitality Association was claiming this could result in up to 45,000 job losses. The Unite union also carried out a campaign and its General Secretary claimed the decision a triumph for the poorly paid. Not everyone agreed. Some thought there should be no tipping at all, as in Australia. Others said the Canadian system was best – wages are low but generous tips are left, and this motivates staff to give excellent service.

a) Look at the table below. In your view, which of the statements are facts and which are opinions? In each case, justify your view.

Statement	Fact or opinion?	Justification
i) Having a national minimum wage helps low-paid workers.		
ii) Over one million people will benefit from the minimum wage increase.		
iii) The new law on tips will stop restaurants paying below minimum wage rates.		
iv) Using the Australian system of no tips would be better.		
v) The Canadian system guarantees good service.		
vi) 45,000 job losses will occur in the hospitality industry.		

b) All newspapers have their own way of putting forward the news. Go to page 104 to see how to access a website which will help you to compare the way that news is reported in different newspapers.

Compare six different newspapers and make notes on:

i) the type of stories covered

ii) the way views are put forward.

Activity: How to go about your research

A lot of scientific research is based upon public opinion. An environmental researcher could use a questionnaire to find out if people use their energy resources efficiently or how good they are at recycling waste. This information could inform a campaign to tell people how to reduce their energy output and prevent damage to the environment.

A quantitative questionnaire such as the one below is the best way to find out what people think. This format allows the researcher to collate the data easily and form a strong conclusion.

Completing the following questionnaire will help you to think about how to produce a survey. You may be required to design a questionnaire as part of the course.

BTEC National in Applied Science (Environmental Science) questionnaire					
WHAT IMPACT DO YOU HAVE ON THE ENVIRONMENT?					
	Circle the answer that applies to you personally: 1 means you are least likely to do it and 5 means you are most likely to do it.				
• I am aware that my own actions affect the environment.	1	2	3	4	5
• I leave lights on in the house.	1	2	3	4	5
• I leave my computer on standby.	1	2	3	4	5
• I leave the TV on standby.	1	2	3	4	5
• I come to lessons in a car.	1	2	3	4	5
• I get the bus to lessons.	1	2	3	4	5
• I often travel abroad.	1	2	3	4	5
• I walk to lessons.	1	2	3	4	5
• I recycle cardboard.	1	2	3	4	5
• I recycle glass.	1	2	3	4	5
• I recycle plastics.	1	2	3	4	5
• I recycle paper.	1	2	3	4	5
Additional information					

TOP TIP

The internet and other data sources are great but, with so much information out there, how do you get to the important stuff? You need a research plan!

Step Nine: Make an effective presentation

Case study: Well-prepared presentations

George, Mahla and Sarah are producing a group presentation for one of their BTEC National Subsidiary Diploma assignments entitled 'Energy for the Future'.

They decide to make a plan of the information they intend to include in their presentation in order to gain a distinction grade. They think about how they will present the information to make sure their classmates find it interesting and easy to understand.

George, Mahla and Sarah include the following points in their plan which ensures that they are well prepared:

- Use PowerPoint size 24 font with black writing to create the presentation.
- Keep writing to a minimum on slides and include referenced diagrams and photographs.
- Include a title, introduction and summary.
- Use bullet points for the main points.
- Include all the information required; use books, internet and journals.
- Make additional notes for each slide to help to answer any questions.

- Decide who will present which slides.
- Rehearse individually and together.
- Practise the presentation several times and give constructive feedback to each other.
- Print handouts for the class and a full set for each of us (use as prompt cards).
- Check the time and place of the presentation, be early and look smart.

Reflection points

Thinking about your own presentation skills, could you present an idea one to one to another learner?

Could you present the same idea to a small group of colleagues?

Given enough time to prepare, could you give a talk to a much larger audience?

What about making a presentation to a group of people you don't know?

Making a presentation can be nerve-wracking. It involves several skills, including planning, preparation and communication. It tests your ability to work in a team, speak in public and use IT (normally PowerPoint). You also have to stay calm under pressure. However, as it is excellent practice for your future, you can expect presentations to be a common method of assessing your performance.

TOP TIP

When you're giving a presentation, keep to time, get to the point and use your time well.

Good planning and preparation

Being well prepared, and rehearsing beforehand, helps your confidence and your presentation. The following points will help you to do this.

- If you're part of a team, find out everyone's strengths and weaknesses and divide work fairly taking these into account. Decide how long each person should speak, who should introduce the team and who will summarise at the end.

- Take into account your time-scale, resources and team skills. A simple, clear presentation is better – and safer – than a complicated one.

- If you're using PowerPoint, make slides more interesting by avoiding a series of bulleted lists and including artwork. Print PowerPoint notes for the audience. Use a fuller set of notes for yourself, as a prompt.

- Check the venue and time.

- Decide what to wear and check it's clean and presentable.

- Prepare, check and print your handouts.

- Decide, as a team, the order in which people will speak, bearing in mind the topic.

- Discuss possible questions and how to answer them.

- Rehearse beforehand to check your timings.

If you prepare properly you can really enjoy giving a presentation.

TOP TIP

Rehearsing properly allows you to speak fluently, just glancing at your notes to remind you of the next key point.

On the day, you can achieve a better performance if you:

- arrive in plenty of time
- calm your nerves by taking deep breaths before going in front of your audience
- introduce yourself clearly, and smile at the audience
- avoid reading from your screen or your notes
- explain what you are going to do – especially if giving a demonstration – do it and then review what you've done
- say you will deal with questions at the end of any demonstration
- answer questions honestly – don't exaggerate, guess or waffle
- respond positively to all feedback, which should be used to improve your performance next time.

TOP TIPS

Make sure you can be heard clearly by lifting your head and speaking a little more slowly and loudly than normal.

Key points

- When making a presentation, prepare well, don't be too ambitious and have several rehearsals.
- When giving a demonstration, explain first what you are going to do and that you will answer questions at the end.

Case study: Learner quotes about making presentations

Most people start off feeling uncomfortable about talking in front of a group of people, whether they know them or not. This is what some real learners have said about having to give presentations as part of their BTEC course.

"I actually feel more comfortable giving a presentation rather than having to write an essay. What I really enjoy about it is the fact that sometimes we have to prepare a presentation as a whole group. I like that we work together to find information and then we take turns presenting different points. The fact that I am not the only one out there and I am part of a supportive team makes it fun for me."
Gabriela, 16, BTEC Level 2 First in Performing Arts

"Although presentations are very stressful, when I present my work it helps to hang my ideas together and I find I can express what I want to say more clearly than when I write things down. Instant feedback is helpful and boosts my confidence for the next time."
Ethan, 19, BTEC Level 2 First in Creative Media Production

"I think presentations are useful but I find them difficult to deliver – relying heavily on my memory, which is very nerve-racking. We were told that presentation would be part of our assessment. I really worried about it and couldn't sleep the night before – stressing out about what I was going to say. I hated the first few minutes, but after that I was OK."
Will, 16, BTEC Level 2 First in Engineering

"I was very nervous about presenting to my class until I took part in the Young Enterprise scheme and had to present the results of our project to over 200 people including the mayor! After that, presenting to my class mates didn't feel too nerve-wracking at all."
Lizzy, 17, BTEC Level 2 First in Business

"I used to dread presentations on my course, but found that if I went through my notes again and again until I knew the presentation inside out, it made it much easier and the presentations generally went well."
Javinder, 17, BTEC Level 3 National in Construction

"I used to hate presenting to other people on my course, until I realised that most of them were as nervous about it as I was!"
Koichi, 21, BTEC Level 3 National in Art and Design

Activity: All right on the night?

Read the following account and answer the questions that follow. If possible, compare ideas with a friend in your class.

Gemma looked around in exasperation. The team were on the final rehearsal of their presentation and nothing was going right. Amaya seemed to think it was funny. 'Honestly, Gemma, why don't you just chill for a bit?' she suggested. 'You know what they say – a bad dress rehearsal means we'll do really well tomorrow!'

Gemma glared at her. 'Well, can I make a suggestion, too, Amaya,' she retorted. 'Why don't you just concentrate for a change? Sprawling around and dissolving into giggles every five minutes isn't helping either.'

She turned to Adam. 'And I thought you were going to build a simple model,' she said, 'not one that falls apart every time you touch it.'

Adam looked crest-fallen. 'But I wanted to show how it worked.'

'How it's supposed to work, you mean!' raged Gemma, all her worries and anxieties now coming to the fore. 'We'll look stupid if it ends up in bits on the floor tomorrow and Amaya just falls about laughing again.'

'And Imran,' continued Gemma, turning her sights on the last member of the team, 'why is it so difficult for you to count to three minutes? We've agreed over and over again we'll each talk for three minutes and every time you get carried away with the sound of your own voice and talk for twice as long. It just means we're going to overrun and get penalised. And stop trying to wriggle out of answering questions properly. For heaven's sake, if you don't know the answer, how hard is it just to say so?'

Silence fell. No-one looked at each other. Adam fiddled with his model and something else fell off. Amaya wanted to laugh but didn't dare.

Imran was sulking and vowed never to say anything ever again. 'You wait,' he thought. 'Tomorrow I'll race through my part in one minute flat. And then what are you going to do?'

1 Identify the strengths and weaknesses of each member of the presentation team.

Name	Strengths	Weaknesses
Gemma		
Amaya		
Adam		
Imran		

2 What has the team done right, so far, in getting ready for the presentation?

3 Why do you think the team is having problems?

4 If you were Gemma's tutor, what advice would you give her at this point?

Activity: What to do in your presentation

Imagine you are giving an individual presentation to a group of work colleagues in the haematology department of your local NHS hospital. Think about the key points you will need to cover. Your presentation is on 'Why do we need to ensure that the correct blood type is used for blood transfusion following surgery'.

Tick the most appropriate box for each of the statements in the table below. For each statement explain why you should or should not do that particular thing.

Statement	Yes	No	Why?
I must give an introduction.			
I should rehearse my presentation beforehand.			
I need to look at the screen when delivering my presentation.			
I don't need to include any pictures or photographs.			
I should cram as much information on each slide as possible.			
I need up-to-date relevant information with evidence.			
I should speak loudly and clearly and look at the audience.			
I need to understand my presentation and read up around it.			
My presentation should last a very long time.			
I should give handouts to each of my colleagues.			
I should put a lot of the information into bullet points.			
I should be on time and prepared for my presentation.			

TOP TIP

When making PowerPoint presentations don't just read out what it says on the slides. The audience can do this. Use the slides as prompt cards.

Step Ten: Maximise your opportunities and manage your problems

Case study: Making the most of opportunities and dealing with problems

Emma is studying for a BTEC Level 3 National Diploma in Applied Science (Medical Science). She really wants to go to university to train for her dream job – teaching Physics. Emma is a very good learner and uses every opportunity on her course to maximise her grades.

As part of the course, Emma completes a work experience placement at a local comprehensive school. She shadows the science technician to get a feel of what it would be like to work in a school environment. During her placement, she asks many questions and makes lots of notes. These help her to complete the assignment that follows the placement.

When a visiting speaker comes to her centre to talk about 'The Universe', Emma makes a list of questions to ask which relate to another assignment. This helps her to get a distinction for that particular assignment.

Although Emma is generally very hardworking, she becomes ill and is off college for two weeks. Emma is too poorly to make any progress on three assignments which makes her very upset and stressed. She phones her tutor who is sympathetic and agrees to give her an extension.

This makes Emma feel much better and, as soon as she fells well enough, she starts to catch up with the work. On Emma's return to college, her tutor gives her the notes for the sessions that she missed and arranges to meet her at lunchtime to go over a new assignment that was given out during her absence.

Later in the course, Emma encounters another problem when her father becomes very ill. Emma is extremely distressed, she finds it hard to concentrate on her work and life at home is very difficult. Emma discusses the situation with her tutor, who refers her to a counsellor. Having someone to speak to really helps Emma to deal with her problems and together they devise a way to help her through the course.

Despite encountering difficulties, Emma receives a distinction grade overall and goes on to university where she is now studying successfully to be a Physics teacher.

Reflection points

Do you have the confidence to make best use of opportunities presented to you?

How do you tackle problems?

If your course takes one or two years to complete, then it is highly likely that you will experience some highs and lows in that time. You may find one or two topics harder than the rest. There may be distractions in your personal life to cope with. All of which means than you may not always be able to do your best.

It is, therefore, sensible to have an action plan to help you cope. It's also wise to plan how to make the best of opportunities for additional experiences or learning. This section shows you how to do this.

TOP TIP

Because life rarely runs smoothly, it's sensible to capitalise on the opportunities that come your way and have a plan to deal with problems.

Making the most of your opportunities

There will be many opportunities for learning on your course, not all of which will be in school or college. You should prepare for some of the following to maximise the opportunities that each offer.

- **External visits**. Prepare in advance by reading about relevant topics. Make notes when you are there. Write up your notes neatly and file them safely for future reference.

- **Visiting speakers**. Questions can usually be submitted to the speaker in advance. Think carefully about information that you would find helpful. Make notes, unless someone has been appointed to make notes for the whole group. You may be asked to thank the speaker on behalf of your group.

- **Work experience**. If work experience is an essential part of your course, your tutor will help you to organise your placement and tell you about the evidence you need to obtain. You may also get a special logbook in which to record your experiences. Read and re-read the units to which your evidence will apply and make sure you understand the grading criteria and what you need to obtain. Make time to write up your notes, logbook and/or diary every night (if possible), while everything is fresh in your mind.

- **In your own workplace**. If you have a full-time or part-time job, watch for opportunities to find out more about relevant topics that relate to your course, such as health and safety, teamwork, dealing with customers, IT security and communications. Your employer will have had to address all of these issues. Finding out more about these issues will broaden your knowledge and give more depth to your assessment responses.

- **Television, newspapers, podcasts and other information sources**. The media can be an invaluable source of information. Look out for news bulletins relating to your studies, as well as information in topical television programmes – from *The Apprentice* to *Top Gear*. You can also read news headlines online. Podcasts are useful, too. It will help if you know what topics you will be studying in the months to come, so you can spot useful opportunities as they arise.

TOP TIP

Remember that you can use online catch-up services, such as the BBC iPlayer or 4oD (for Channel 4 shows) to see TV programmes you have missed recently.

Minimising problems

Hopefully, any problems you experience during your course will only be minor; such as struggling to find an acceptable working method with someone in your team.

You should already know who to talk to about these issues, and who to go to if that person is absent or you would prefer to talk to someone else. If your problems are affecting your work, it's sensible to see your tutor promptly. It is a rare learner who is enthusiastic about every topic and gets on well with everyone else doing the course, so your tutor won't be surprised and will give you useful guidance (in confidence) to help.

TOP TIP

Don't delay talking to someone in confidence if you have a serious problem. If your course tutor is unavailable, talk to another staff member you like and trust.

Other sources of help

If you are unfortunate enough to have a more serious personal problem, the following sources of help may be available in your centre.

- **Professional counselling.** There may be a professional counselling service. If you see a counsellor, nothing you say during the session can be mentioned to another member of staff without your permission.

- **Complaint procedures.** If you have a serious complaint, the first step is to talk to your tutor. If you can't resolve your problem informally, there will be a formal learner complaint procedure. These procedures are used only for serious issues, not for minor difficulties.

- **Appeals procedures.** If you disagree with your final grade for an assignment, check the grading criteria and ask the subject tutor to explain how the grade was awarded. If you are still unhappy, talk to your personal tutor. If you still disagree, you have the right to make a formal appeal.

- **Disciplinary procedures.** These exist for when learners consistently flout a centre's rules and ensure that all learners are dealt with in the same way. Hopefully, you will never get into trouble, but you should make sure that you read these procedures carefully to see what could happen if you did. Remember that being honest and making a swift apology is always the wisest course of action.

- **Serious illness.** Whether this involves you, a family member or a close friend, it could affect your attendance. Discuss the problem with your tutor promptly; you will be missing information from the first day you are absent. There are many solutions in this type of situation – such as sending notes by post and updating you electronically (providing you are well enough to cope with the work).

TOP TIP

It's important to know your centre's procedures for dealing with important issues such as complaints, major illnesses, learner appeals and disciplinary matters.

Key points

- Don't miss opportunities to learn more about relevant topics through external visits, listening to visiting speakers, work experience, being at work or even watching television.
- If you have difficulties or concerns, talk to your tutor, or another appropriate person, promptly to make sure your work isn't affected.

Action points

1 Prepare in advance to maximise your opportunities.
   a) List the opportunities available on your course for obtaining more information and talking to experts. You can check with your tutor to make sure you've identified them all.
   b) Check the content of each unit you will be studying so that you know the main topics and focus of each.
   c) Identify the information that may be relevant to your course on television, on radio, in newspapers and in podcasts.

2 Make sure you know how to cope if you have a serious problem.
   a) Check your centre's procedures so you know who to talk to in a crisis, and who to contact if that person is absent.
   b) Find out where you can get hold of a copy of the main procedures in your centre that might affect you if you have a serious problem. Then read them.

Activity: What to do if problems occur

During your BTEC Level 3 National in Applied Science course you may, at some time, encounter a problem. Being prepared by making notes on who to contact and what to do will help to you to complete your course and be successful in any future science-related study and career.

1 Complete the following table with the information that applies to your centre.

Who should I contact if:	Person to contact and what to do
I am off ill?	
I have a problem with any of my work?	
I have a personal problem?	
I don't agree with the grade I have been given for one of my assignments?	
I am in trouble for something (eg lateness, not handing in work, poor attendance, plagiarism or general bad behaviour)?	

2 You will probably go on one or more visits during your course. You might visit a variety of places involved with science. This is really useful as you can see how different scientists work, and the career opportunities that are open to you as a scientist.

Answer the following questions to help you prepare for a visit to a local university. Final-year degree students and PhD students will show you around the different laboratories where scientific research is being undertaken.

What essential equipment should you take with you on the visit?

What information could you collect and how should you collect it?

AND FINALLY ...

Refer to this Study Skills Guide whenever you need to remind yourself about something related to your course. Keep it in a safe place so that you can use it whenever you need to refresh your memory. That way, you'll get the very best out of your course – and yourself!

Your Study Skills Guide will help you gain the skills you need for success.

Skills building

This section has been written to help you improve the skills needed to do your best in your assignments. You may be excellent at some skills already, others may need further work. The skills you can expect to demonstrate on your course include:

- your personal, learning and thinking skills (**PLTS**)
- your **functional skills** of ICT, maths/numeracy and English
- your proofreading and document production skills.

Personal, learning and thinking skills (PLTS)

These are the skills, personal qualities and behaviour that enable you to operate more independently, work more confidently with other people and be more effective at work. You'll develop these on your BTEC Level 3 National course through a variety of experiences and as you take on different roles and responsibilities.

The skills are divided into six groups:

1 **Independent enquirers** can process and evaluate information they investigate from different perspectives. They can plan what to do and how to do it, and take into account the consequences of making different decisions.

2 **Creative thinkers** generate and explore different ideas. They make connections between ideas, events and experiences that enable them to be inventive and imaginative.

3 **Reflective learners** can assess themselves and other people. They can evaluate their own strengths and limitations. They set themselves realistic goals, monitor their own performance and welcome feedback.

4 **Team workers** collaborate with other people to achieve common goals. They are fair and considerate to others, whether as a team leader or team member, and take account of different opinions.

5 **Self-managers** are well-organised and show personal responsibility, initiative, creativity and enterprise. They look for new challenges and responsibilities and are flexible when priorities change.

6 **Effective participators** play a full part in the life of their school, college, workplace or wider community by taking responsible action to bring improvements for others as well as themselves.

Action points

1 Many parts of this Study Skills Guide relate to the development of your own personal, learning and thinking skills. For each of the following, suggest the main skill groups to which the chapter relates. Refer to the box above and write a number next to each chapter title below.

a) Use your time wisely. ____

b) Understand how to research and analyse information. ____

c) Work productively as a member of a group. ____

d) Understand yourself. ____

e) Utilise all your resources. ____

f) Maximise your opportunities and manage your problems. ____

2 You have been on your BTEC National course for a few months now and, although everyone is enjoying the work, you realise that some of the learners have complaints.

Firstly, several learners object to an increase in the price of printouts and photocopying, on the basis that they can't do good work for their assignments if this is too expensive. You disagree and think that the prices are reasonable, given the cost of paper.

Secondly, a timetable change means your 2 pm – 4 pm Friday afternoon class has been moved to 9 am – 11 am. Some learners are annoyed and want it changed back, while others are delighted.

a) For the first problem, identify four factors which could indicate that those complaining about the price rise might be justified.

1

2

3

4

b) For the second problem:
   i) Think about which learners in your group would be most affected by the timetable change. Who might be most disturbed? Who might benefit from the earlier start?
   ii) Try to think of a creative solution, or compromise, that would please both groups.

c) During the discussions about these issues, some quieter members of the class are often shouted down by the more excitable members. Suggest a strategy for dealing with this, which everyone is likely to accept.

You can also check your ideas with the suggestions given on page 103.

3 a) Complete the chart opposite, identifying occasions when you may need to demonstrate personal, learning and thinking skills in your future career. Alternatively, apply each area to a part-time job you are currently doing.

b) Identify areas where you think you are quite strong and put a tick in the 'S' column. Check that you could provide evidence to support this judgement, such as a time when you have demonstrated this skill.

c) Now consider areas where you are not so good and put a cross in the 'W' column.

d) Then practise self-management by identifying two appropriate goals to achieve over the next month and make a note of them in the space provided. If possible, talk through your ideas at your next individual tutorial.

Personal, learning and thinking skills for future career/current part-time job				
Skill group	**Example skills**	**Occasions when you use/ will use skill**	**S**	**W**
Independent enquirers	Finding information Solving problems Making decisions Reconciling conflicting information or views Justifying decisions			
Creative thinkers	Finding imaginative solutions Making original connections Finding new ways to do something Opportunities for being innovative and inventive			
Reflective learners	Goals you may set yourself Reviewing your own progress Encouraging feedback Dealing with setbacks or criticism			
Team workers	Working with others Coping with different views to your own Adapting your behaviour Being fair and considerate			
Self-managers	Being self-starting and showing initiative Dealing positively with changing priorities Organising your own time and resources Dealing with pressure Managing your emotions			
Effective participators	Identifying issues of concern to others Proposing ways forward Identifying improvements for others Influencing other people Putting forward a persuasive argument			
Goals	1			
	2			

Functional skills

Functional skills are practical skills that everyone needs to have in order to study and work effectively. They involve using and applying English, maths and ICT.

Improving your literacy skills

Your written English communication skills

A good vocabulary increases your ability to explain yourself clearly. Work that is presented without spelling and punctuation errors looks professional, and increases the likelihood of someone understanding your intended meaning. Your written communication skills will be tested in many assignments. You should work at improving areas of weakness, such as spelling, punctuation or vocabulary.

Try the following to help you improve your written communication skills:

- Read more as this introduces you to new words, and it will help your spelling.
- Look up new words in a dictionary and try to use them in conversation.
- Use a Thesaurus (you can access one electronically in Word) to find alternatives to words you use a lot, this adds variety to your work.
- Never use words you don't understand in the hope that they sound impressive.
- Write neatly, so people can read what you've written.
- Do crosswords to improve your word power and spelling.
- Improve your punctuation – especially the use of apostrophes – either by using an online programme or by using a communication textbook.
- Go to page 104 to see how to gain access to some helpful websites.

Verbal and non-verbal communication (NVC) skills

Talking appropriately means using the right words and 'tone'; using the right body language means sending positive signals to reinforce this message – such as smiling at someone when you say 'Hello'. Both verbal and non-verbal communication skills are essential when dealing with people at work.

The following are some hints for successful communication:

- Be polite, tactful and sensitive to other people's feelings.
- Think about the words and phrases that you like to hear, and use them when communicating with other people.
- Use simple language so that people can understand you easily. Explain what you mean, when necessary.
- Speak at the right pace. Don't speak so slowly that everyone loses interest, or so fast that no-one can understand you.
- Speak loudly enough for people to hear you clearly – but don't shout!
- Think about the specific needs of different people – whether you are talking to a senior manager, an important client, a shy colleague or an angry customer.
- Recognise the importance of non-verbal communication (NVC) so that you send positive signals by smiling, making eye contact, giving an encouraging nod or leaning forwards to show interest.
- Read other people's body language to spot if they are anxious or impatient so that you can react appropriately.

TOP TIP

Make sure you use the right tone for the person you're talking to. Would you talk to an adult in the same way you'd talk to a very young child?

Action points

1 Go to page 104 to see how to gain access to websites which can help you to improve your literacy skills.

2 A battery made in China contained the following information.

> **DO NOT CONNECT IMPROPERLY**
>
> **CHARGE OR DISPOSE OF IN FIRE**

a) Can you see any problems with this? Give a reason for your answer.

b) Reword the information so that it is unambiguous.

3 If you ever thought you could completely trust the spellchecker on your computer, type the text given in box A on the next page into your computer. Your spellchecker will not highlight a single error; yet even at a glance you should be able to spot dozens of errors!

Read the passage in box A and try to understand it. Then rewrite it in box B on the next page without spelling, grammatical or punctuation errors. Compare your finished work with the suggested version on page 103.

Box A

Anyone desirable to write books or reports, be they short or long, should strive too maximise they're optimal use of one's English grammar and obliviously there is an need for correct spelling two one should not neglect punctuation neither.

Frequent lea, many people and individuals become confusing or just do not no it, when righting, when words that mean different, when sounding identically, or when pronounced very similar, are knot too bee spelled inn the same whey. The quay two suck seeding is dew care, a lack off witch Leeds too Miss Spellings that mite otherwise of bean a voided. Spell chequers donut find awl missed takes.

Despite all the pitfalls how ever, with practise, patients and the right altitude, any one can soon become a grate writer and speaker, as what I did.

Box B Now rewrite the passage in the space below without errors.

4 In each of the statements listed in the table below, suggest what the body language described might mean.

Statement	What might this body language mean?
a) You are talking to your manager when he steps away from you and crosses his arms over his chest.	
b) You are talking to your friend about what she did at the weekend but she's avoiding making eye contact with you.	
c) During a tutorial session, your tutor is constantly tapping his fingers on the arm of his chair.	
d) Whenever you talk to your friend about your next assignment she bites her lower lip.	

Improving your maths or numeracy skills

If you think numeracy isn't relevant to you, then think again! Numeracy is an essential life skill. If you can't carry out basic calculations accurately then you will have problems, perhaps when you least expect them. You'll often encounter numbers in various contexts – sometimes they will be correctly given, sometimes not. Unless you have a basic understanding about numeracy, you won't be able to tell the difference.

Good numeracy skills will improve your ability to express yourself, especially in assignments and at work. If you have problems, there are strategies that you can practise to help:

- Do basic calculations in your head, then check them on a calculator.
- Ask your tutor for help if important calculations give you problems.
- When you are using your computer, use the onscreen calculator (or a spreadsheet package) to do calculations.
- Investigate puzzle sites and brain training software, such as Dr Kageyama's Maths Training by Nintendo.

Action points

1 Go to page 104 to see how to gain access to websites which can help you to improve your numeracy skills.

2 Try the following task with a friend or family member.

   Each of you should write down 36 simple calculations in a list, e.g. 8 × 6, 19 − 8, 14 + 6. Exchange lists. See who can answer the most calculations correctly in the shortest time.

3 Figures aren't always what they appear to be. For example, Sophie watches *Who Wants To Be A Millionaire?* She hears Chris Tarrant say that there have been over 500 shows, with 1200 contestants who have each won over £50,000 on average. Five people have won £1 million.

Sophie says she is going to enter because she is almost certain to win more than £50,000 and could even win a million pounds.

a) On the figures given, what is the approximate total of money won over 500 shows (to the nearest £ million)?

b) Assuming that Sophie is chosen to appear on the show, and makes it on air as a contestant, do you think Sophie's argument that she will 'almost certainly' win more than £50,000 is correct? Give a reason for your answer. (The correct answer is on page 104.)

4 You have a part-time job and have been asked to carry out a survey on the usage of the drinks vending machine. You decide to survey 500 people, and find that:
- 225 use the machine to buy one cup of coffee per day only
- 100 use the machine to buy one cup of tea per day only
- 75 use the machine to buy one cup of cold drink per day only
- 50 use the machine to buy one cup of hot chocolate per day only
- the rest are non-users
- the ratio of male to female users is 2:1.

a) How many men in your survey use the machine?

b) How many women in your survey use the machine?

c) Calculate the proportion of the people in your survey that use the machine. Express this as a fraction and as a percentage.

d) What is the ratio of coffee drinkers to tea drinkers in your survey?

e) What is the ratio of coffee drinkers to hot chocolate drinkers in your survey?

f) If people continue to purchase from the machine in the same ratio found in your survey, and last month 1800 cups of coffee were sold, what would you expect the sales of the cold drinks to be?

g) Using the answer to f), if coffee costs 65p and all cold drinks cost 60p, how much would have been spent in total last month on these two items?

Improving your ICT skills

Good ICT skills are an asset in many aspects of your daily life and not just for those studying to be IT practitioners.

The following are ways in which you can Improve your ICT skills:

- Check that you can use the main features of the software packages you need to produce your assignments, eg Word, Excel and PowerPoint.
- Choose a good search engine and learn to use it properly. For more information, go to page 104 to see how to access a useful website.
- Developing and using your IT skills enables you to enhance your assignments. This may include learning how to import and export text and artwork from one package to another; taking digital photographs and inserting them into your work and/or creating drawings or diagrams by using appropriate software.

Action points

1 Check your basic knowledge of IT terminology by identifying each of these items on your computer screen:

a) taskbar

b) toolbar

c) title bar

d) menu bar

e) mouse pointer

f) scroll bars

g) status bar

h) insertion point

i) maximise/minimise button.

2 Assess your IT skills by identifying the packages and operations you find easy to use and those that you find more difficult. If you use Microsoft Office products (Word, PowerPoint, Access or Excel) you can find out more about improving your skills online. Go to page 104 for information on how to access a useful website.

3 Search the internet to find a useful dictionary of IT terms. Bookmark it for future use. Find out the meaning of any of the following terms that you don't know already:

a) portal

b) cached link

c) home page

d) browser

e) firewall

f) HTML

g) URL

h) cookie

i) hyperlink

j) freeware.

Proofreading and document preparation skills

Improving your keyboard, document production and general IT skills can save you hours of time. When you have good skills, the work you produce will be of a far more professional standard.

- Think about learning to touch type. Your centre may have a workshop you can join, or you can use an online program – go to page 104 to see how you can access websites that will allow you to test and work on improving your typing skills.

- Obtain correct examples of any document formats you will have to use, such as a report or summary, either from your tutor, the internet or from a textbook.

- Proofread all your work carefully. A spellchecker won't find all your mistakes, so you must read through it yourself as well.

- Make sure your work looks professional by using a suitable typeface and font size, as well as reasonable margins.

- Print your work and store the printouts neatly, so that it stays in perfect condition for when you hand it in.

Action points

1 You can check and improve your typing skills using online typing sites – see link in previous section.

2 Check your ability to create documents by scoring yourself out of 5 for each of the following questions, where 5 is something you can do easily and 0 is something you can't do at all. Then focus on improving every score where you rated yourself 3 or less.

I know how to:

a) create a new document and open a saved document _____

b) use the mouse to click, double-click and drag objects _____

c) use drop-down menus _____

d) customise my toolbars by adding or deleting options _____

e) save and/or print a document _____

f) create folders and sub-folders to organise my work _____

g) move a folder I use regularly to My Places _____

h) amend text in a document _____

i) select, copy, paste and delete information in a document _____

j) quickly find and replace text in a document _____

k) insert special characters _____

l) create a table or insert a diagram in a document _____

m) change the text size, font and colour _____

n) add bold, italics or underscore _____

o) create a bullet or numbered list _____

p) align text left, right or centred _____

q) format pages before they are printed _____

r) proofread a document so that there are no mistakes _____.

Answers

Activity: Let's give you a tip... (page 80)

a) i)   Fact
   ii) Opinion – the number cannot be validated
   iii) Fact
   iv) Opinion
   v)   Opinion
   vi) Opinion – again the number is estimated

Skills building answers

PLTS action points (page 93)

1 a) Use your time wisely = **5** Self-managers
  b) Understand how to research and analyse information = **1** Independent enquirers, **5** Self-managers
  c) Work productively as a member of a group = **4** Team workers, **6** Effective participators
  d) Understand yourself = **3** Reflective learners
  e) Utilise all your resources = **5** Self-managers
  f) Maximise your opportunities and manage your problems = **1** Independent enquirers, **2** Creative thinkers, **3** Reflective learners, **5** Self-managers

2 a) Factors to consider in relation to the increased photocopying/printing charges include: the comparative prices charged by other schools/colleges, how often there is a price rise, whether any printing or photocopying at all can be done without charge, whether there are any concessions for special tasks or assignments, the availability of class sets of books/popular library books for loan (which reduces the need for photocopying).

b) i) An earlier start will be more likely to negatively affect those who live further away and who are reliant on public transport, particularly in rural areas. The earlier finish will benefit anyone who has a part-time job that starts on a Friday afternoon or who has after college commitments, such as looking after younger sisters or brothers.

   ii) The scope for compromise would depend on whether there are any classes between 11 am and 2 pm on a Friday, whether tutors had any flexibility and whether the new 9 am – 11 am class could be moved to another time or day.

c) One strategy would be to allow discussion for a set time, ensure everyone had spoken, then put the issue to a vote. The leader should prompt suggestions from quieter members by asking people individually what they think.

Literacy skills action points (page 97)

2 a) The statement reads as if it is acceptable to either charge it or dispose of it in fire.
  b) Do not connect this battery improperly. Do not recharge it and do not dispose of it in fire.

3 Anyone who wishes to write books or reports, whether short or long, should try to use English grammatically. Obviously there is a need for correct spelling, too. Punctuation should also not be neglected.

Frequently, people confuse words with different meanings when they are writing, especially when these sound identical or very similar, even when they must not be spelled in the same way. The key to succeeding is due care, a lack of which leads to misspellings that might otherwise have been avoided. Spellcheckers do not find all mistakes.

Despite all the pitfalls, however, with practice, patience and the right attitude, anyone can soon become a great writer and speaker, like me.

4 (Possible answers)

a) Stepping backwards and crossing arms across the chest might indicate that your manager is creating a barrier between you and himself or that he is angry.

b) Your friend might be feeling guilty about what she did at the weekend or not confident that you will approve of what she tells you.

c) Your tutor might be frustrated as he has many things to do and so wants the tutorial to be over quickly.

d) Your friend might be anxious about the next assignment or about the time she has to complete it.

Numeracy action points (page 100)

3 a) £60 million

b) Sophie's argument is incorrect as £50,000 is an average, i.e. some contestants will win more, but many will win less. The distribution of prizes is greater at lower amounts because more people win small amounts of money than large amounts – and only five have won the top prize of £1 million.

4 a) 300

b) 150

c) 9/10ths, 90%

d) 225:100 (= 45:20) = 9:4

e) 225:50 = 9:2

f) 600

g) £1530

Accessing website links

Links to various websites are referred to throughout this BTEC Level 3 National Study Skills Guide. To ensure that these links are up-to-date, that they work and that the sites aren't inadvertently linked to any material that could be considered offensive, we have made the links available on our website: www.pearsonhotlinks.co.uk. When you visit the site, search for either the title BTEC Level 3 National Study Skills Guide in Applied Science or ISBN 9781846905636. From here you can gain access to the website links and information on how they can be used to help you with your studies.

Useful terms

Accreditation of Prior Learning (APL)
Some of your previous achievements and experiences may be able to be used to count towards your qualification.

Apprenticeships
Schemes that enable you to work and earn money at the same time as you gain further qualifications (an NVQ award and a technical certificate) and improve your functional skills. Apprentices learn work-based skills relevant to their job role and their chosen industry. See page 104 for information on how to access a website where you can find out more.

Assessment methods
Techniques used to check that your work demonstrates the learning and understanding required for your qualification, such as assignments, case studies and practical tasks.

Assessor
An assessor is the tutor who marks or assesses your work.

Assignment
A complex task or mini-project set to meet specific grading criteria and learning outcomes.

Awarding body
An organisation responsible for devising, assessing and issuing qualifications. The awarding body for all BTEC qualifications is Edexcel.

Credit value
The number of credits attached to your BTEC course. The credit value increases in relation to the length of time you need to complete the course, from 30 credits for a BTEC Level 3 Certificate, 60 credits for a Subsidiary Diploma, 120 credits for a Diploma, up to 180 credits for an Extended Diploma.

Degrees
Higher education qualifications offered by universities and colleges. Foundation degrees take two years to complete; honours degrees may take three years or longer.

Department for Business Innovation and Skills (BIS)
BIS is responsible for further and higher education and skills training, as well as functions related to trade and industry. See page 104 for information on accessing a website to find out more.

Department for Education
The Department for Education is the government department responsible for schools and education, as well as for children's services.

Distance learning
When you learn and/or study for a qualification at home or at work. You communicate with your tutor and/or the centre that organises the course by post, telephone or electronically.

Educational Maintenance Award (EMA)
An EMA is a means-tested award that provides eligible learners under 19, who are studying a full-time course at school or college, with a cash sum of money every week. See page 104 for information on how to access a website where you can find out more.

External verification
Formal checking of the programme by an Edexcel representative that focuses on sampling various assignments to check content, accurate assessment and grading.

Forbidden combinations
There are some qualifications that cannot be taken simultaneously because their content is too similar.

Functional skills
Practical skills in English, maths and ICT that enable people to work confidently, effectively and independently. Level 2 Functional Skills are mapped to the units of BTEC Level 3 National qualifications. They aren't compulsory to achieve on the course, but are of great use.

Grade boundaries
Pre-set points that determine whether you will achieve a pass, merit or distinction as the overall final grade(s) for your qualification.

Grading criteria
The specific evidence you have to demonstrate to obtain a particular grade in the unit.

Grading domains
The main areas of learning that support the learning outcomes. On a BTEC Level 3 National course these are: application of knowledge and understanding; development of practical and technical skills; personal development for occupational roles; application of PLTS and functional skills.

Grading grid
The table in each unit of your qualification specification that sets out what you have to show you can do.

Higher education (HE)
Post-secondary and post-further education, usually provided by universities and colleges.

Higher-level skills
These are skills such as evaluating or critically assessing information. They are more difficult than lower-level skills such as writing a description or making a list. You must be able to demonstrate higher-level skills to achieve a distinction.

Indicative reading
Recommended books and journals whose content is both suitable and relevant for the BTEC unit studied.

Induction
A short programme of events at the start of a course designed to give you essential information, and introduce you to your fellow learners and tutors, so that you can settle down as quickly and easily as possible.

Internal verification
The quality checks carried out by nominated tutors at your school or college to ensure that all assignments are at the right level, cover appropriate learning outcomes and grading criteria, and that all assessors are marking work consistently and to the same standard.

Investors in People (IiP)
A national quality standard that sets a level of good practice for training and developing of people within a business. Participating organisations must demonstrate commitment to achieve the standard.

Learning outcomes
The knowledge and skills you must demonstrate to show that you have effectively learned a unit.

Learning support
Additional help that is available to all learners in a school or college who have learning difficulties or other special needs.

Levels of study
The depth, breadth and complexity of knowledge, understanding and skills required to achieve a qualification, which also determines its level. Level 2 equates to GCSE level and Level 3 equates to A-level. As you successfully achieve one level, you can then progress to the next. BTEC qualifications are offered at Entry Level, then Levels 1, 2, 3, 4 and 5.

Local Education Authority (LEA)
The local government body responsible for providing education for all learners of compulsory school age. The LEA is also responsible for managing the education budget for 16–19 learners in its area.

Mandatory units
These are units that all learners must complete to gain a qualification; in this case a BTEC Level 3 National. Some BTEC qualifications have an over-arching title, eg Construction, but within Construction you can choose different pathways. Your chosen pathway may have additional mandatory units specific to that pathway.

Mentor
A more experienced person who will guide you, and counsel you if you have a problem or difficulty.

Mode of delivery
The way in which a qualification is offered to learners for example, part-time, full-time, as a short course or by distance learning.

National Occupational Standard (NOS)
Statements of the skills, knowledge and understanding you need to develop in order to be competent at a particular job.

National Vocational Qualification (NVQ)
Qualifications that concentrate on the practical skills and knowledge required to do a job competently. They are usually assessed in the workplace and range from Level 1 (the lowest) to Level 5 (the highest).

Nested qualifications

Qualifications that have 'common' units, so that learners can easily progress from one to another by adding on more units.

Ofqual

The public body responsible for regulating qualifications, exams and tests in England.

Optional units

Units on your course from which you may be able to make a choice. They help you specialise your skills, knowledge and understanding and may help progression into work or further education.

Pathway

All BTEC Level 3 National qualifications comprise a small number of mandatory units and a larger number of optional units. These units are grouped into different combinations to provide alternative pathways to achieving the qualification. These pathways are usually linked to different career preferences.

Peer review

This involves feedback on your performance by your peers (members of your team, or class group.) You will also be given an opportunity to review their performance.

Plagiarism

The practice of copying someone else's work, or work from any other sources (eg the internet), and passing it off as your own. This practice is strictly forbidden on all courses.

Personal, learning and thinking skills (PLTS)

The skills, personal qualities and behaviour that improve your ability to work independently. Developing these skills makes you more effective and confident at work. Opportunities for developing these skills are a feature of all BTEC Level 3 National courses. These skills aren't compulsory to achieve on the course, but are of great use to you.

Portfolio

A collection of work compiled by a learner, usually as evidence of learning, to present to an assessor.

Procrastinator

Someone who is forever putting off or delaying work, either because they are lazy or because they have poor organisational skills.

Professional body

An organisation that exists to promote or support a particular profession; for example, the Royal Institute of British Architects (RIBA).

Professional development and training

This involves undertaking activities relevant to your job to increase and/or update your knowledge and skills.

Project

A project is a comprehensive piece of work, which normally involves original research and investigation by an individual or by a team. The findings and results may be presented in writing and summarised as a presentation.

Qualifications and Credit Framework (QCF)

The QCF is a framework for recognising skills and qualifications. It does this by awarding credit for qualifications and units so that they are easier to measure and compare. All BTEC Level 3 National qualifications are part of the QCF.

Qualifications and Curriculum Development Agency (QCDA)

The QCDA is responsible for maintaining and developing the national curriculum, delivering assessments, tests and examinations and reforming qualifications.

Quality assurance

In education, this is the process of continually checking that a course of study is meeting the specific requirements set down by the awarding body.

Sector Skills Councils (SSCs)

The 25 employer-led, independent organisations responsible for improving workforce skills in the UK by identifying skills gaps and improving learning in the workplace. Each council covers a different type of industry.

Semester

Many universities and colleges divide their academic year into two halves or semesters, one from September to January and one from February to July.

Seminar

A learning event involving a group of learners and a tutor, which may be learner-led, and follow research into a topic that has been introduced at an earlier stage.

Study buddy

A person in your group or class who takes notes for you and keeps you informed of important developments if you are absent. You do the same for them in return.

Time-constrained assignment

An assessment you must complete within a fixed time limit.

Tutorial

An individual or small group meeting with your tutor at which you can discuss your current work and other more general course issues. At an individual tutorial, your progress on the course will be discussed and you can raise any concerns or personal worries you may have.

The University and Colleges Admissions Service (UCAS)

UCAS (pronounced 'you-cass') is the central organisation that processes all applications for higher education (HE) courses.

UCAS points

The number of points allocated by UCAS for the qualifications you have obtained. Higher education institutions specify how many points you need to be accepted on the courses they offer. See page 104 for information on how to access a website where you can find out more.

Unit abstract

The summary at the start of each BTEC unit that tells you what the unit is about.

Unit content

Details about the topics covered by the unit and the knowledge and skills you need to complete it.

Unit points

The number of points you gain when you complete a unit. These will depend on the grade you achieve (pass, merit or distinction).

Vocational qualification

Designed to develop knowledge and understanding relevant to a chosen area of work.

Work experience

Time you spend on an employer's premises when you learn about the enterprise, carry out work-based tasks and develop skills and knowledge.

Please note that all information given within these useful terms was correct at the time of going to print.